mo'urban

DICTIONAR

wizard

An exclamation of joy, similar to "cool" or "great." Origins are unknown, but it is featured heavily in the book *Lord of the Flies*.

"We can use Piggy's specs to make a fire!"

"Wizard!"

food baby

When you eat so much your stomach looks pregnant.

Jeez! I ate so much, I look like I am having a food baby!

sea monkey

Little brine shrimp that come with a variety of different tanks. Basically the coolest thing ever. They can live for a long time, and they get their groove on and have baby sea monkeys.

My sea monkeys are so much cooler than yours.

My sea monkeys are mating!

You ass! You dumped my sea monkeys down the drain!

fun bags

Slang word for womens' breasts, such as tits, boobies, hooters, and so on.

Look at the fun bags on that girl.

stink-eye

A dirty look.

She was giving me the stink-eye

I was getting nothing but stink-eye from him.

do me a solid

A different way of saying, "do me a favor."

I want to date this hot chick, but she wants to bring her not-so-hot friend. Can you do me a solid and go out with her friend?

totally boss

Something that is beyond regular awesome.

Guy 1: Man, I'm so glad I went to that concert last night.

Guy 2: Yeah, it was totally boss.

homeskillet

Friend.

Word up, my homeskillet.

shenanigans

Another word for pranks or jokes. When people are messing around and tricking people, it is often referred to as a shenanigan.

Our shenanigans are fun and original, while theirs are cheesy and lame.

JUNO EDITION

mo'urban

DICTIONARY

RIDONKULOUS
STREET SLANG DEFINED

COMPILED BY AARON PECKHAM,
CREATOR OF URBANDICTIONARY.COM

**Andrews McMeel
Publishing, LLC**

Kansas City

Mo' Urban Dictionary

ISBN-13: 978-0-7407-7772-1
ISBN-10: 0-7407-7772-6

www.andrewsmcmeel.com

www.urbandictionary.com

Book design by Diane Marsh

ATTENTION: SCHOOLS AND BUSINESSES

Andrews McMeel books are available at quantity discounts with bulk
purchase for educational, business, or sales promotional use. For information, please
write to: Special Sales Department, Andrews McMeel Publishing, LLC,
4520 Main Street, Kansas City, Missouri 64111.

SHOUT-OUTS

Big shouts to everyone who has helped Urban Dictionary grow. High-fives to Dr. Bensky and my Cal Poly professors; props to my editors at Andrews McMeel in Kansas City; much respect to my coworkers and fellow leet hackers in the yay area; holler to the ACLU; daps to my BFFs, Mike D. and Dave G.; thx to my crew, Sheila and Anna; and much love to my parents, Doug and Brenda, whose work inspires me.

Big ups to the thousands of people who edit urbandictionary.com and to the millions of people who write it.

Holla back,
Aaron Peckham

Introduction

Urban Dictionary is more than a dictionary—it's a catalog of popular culture you helped write. Since it started in 1999, all of its definitions have been written by people like you who visited urbandictionary.com. Thousands of definitions are submitted every day, and many of them get published online. Because it's written by normal people, Urban Dictionary is an opinionated, honest, and sometimes raunchy catalog of the world—from "urban cougar" (an older woman who goes clubbing to hit on younger men) to "pregret" (the feeling of impending regret for something you're going to do anyway).

Urban Dictionary started as the anti-dictionary, a parody of dictionary.com. Today it's not just a parody: Parents and teachers use it to understand the next generation, and you can use it to decode the newest hip-hop lyrics or laugh at "podestrians" and "bluetools." In a UK court case, a judge referred to Urban Dictionary in a lawsuit between two rappers. It's been referenced in trademark disputes, high school graduation speeches, and newspaper articles. Today Urban Dictionary is off the hook: fifty million people visited urbandictionary.com in 2006, and in the last eight years people sent in more than two million definitions.

By publishing your definitions, Urban Dictionary puts the power of the dictionary where it belongs—in the hands of normal people who speak everyday language. Definitions don't always agree—many words are defined differently by different people—but on urbandictionary.com that's totally cool. Wikipedia says it well: "Urban Dictionary allows for many truths, rather than an authoritative guide." This book is a collection of the best of those truths—and you can always find the newest entries online.

My ear is to the ground listening for the word on the street, from "ghost ride the whip" to "sneeze tease" to Nancy Pelosi's "marble ceiling." But I've only got two ears and it's a big world, so Urban Dictionary needs your help—when you hear the newest slang, spread the word, and define your world, at urbandictionary.com.

12th man

In football, the crowd. When the away team is backed up near the goal post, the 12th man makes a lot of noise, making it hard for the lineman to hear the snap count.

Sweet! Seattle just won because the 12th man made the offense commit five false-start penalties.

16

In rap, one verse or sixteen lines.

He had the hottest 16 on Track 2.

$500 lane

The breakdown lane on a highway. Why? Because that's how much money you gotta pay if a cop catches you driving in it. (Can also mean the leftmost lane for trucks when they are only allowed to drive on the right.)

Passenger: This traffic sux! Let's take the $500 lane.

Driver: OK, but only if you'll front the $500 when statey sees us.

5-second rule

An unwritten law dictating that if a food or other consumable item is dropped onto the floor, it may be picked up and eaten within five seconds. The reasoning behind this is that dirt and germs take six seconds to transfer from one surface to another.

Oops, dropped my Popsicle. Five-second rule! (Proceeds to pick up dirty-ass rocket pop and suck the lint off of it.)

68

A sexual favor performed by someone without receiving the favor in return.

Man: Hey, baby, how about we 69?

Woman: How about we 68?

Man: Huh?

Woman: That's where you do me and I owe ya one.

72

Three days off in a row.

I'm taking a 72 this weekend.

8008135

A way to spell "boobies" so no one knows what it is, usually indicating porn or pictures of boobies. Used by computer nerds.

Look! Fresh 8008135.

831

I love you: 8 letters, 3 words, 1 meaning.

Shout out to Scott! 831 babe!

9/11 Republican

A person who usually voted Democratic, but has been taken in by the Bush administration's fear-mongering.

I thought my dad was going to vote for Kerry, but he turned out to be another 9/11 Republican.

9 to 9

Way to say "You hustle." Most people work from 9 to 5, but you put in more. You have the 9 to 9 hustle.

I've decided to bid adieu to the 9 to 9 grind.

@gmail.com

The only suffix to your name that supersedes PhD.

My name is John Smith, MBA, P. Eng, @gmail.com.

AAA

The guy who gets the high score in all the arcade games across the country.

No one's gonna beat AAA's high score in Street Fighter.

AB

Ass-backward, behind the times, not modern.

Man this state is AB! I can't even find a 7-Eleven.

abandominium

An abandoned house that homeless people squat in.

My parents kicked me out, so I'm staying in an abandominium for now.

abc sex

Sex only on anniversaries, birthdays, and Christmas.

They've been married so long they only have abc sex.

absoserious

Absolutely serious, but shorter. We all like short words when we want to be cute.

Benny: Are you sure that you want to break my heart?!

Joon: I am absoserious!

absurdicus

Absurd and ridiculous at the same time; insane.

Will you stop being so absurdicus?

abusage

A hybrid of "usage" and "abuse."

You have committed such a heinous crime of abusage with my alcohol.

abusement

Deriving amusement from the abuse of others; amusement at the expense of others.

You are all here for my abusement.

AC

Air-conditioning, most usually used while driving.

Turn the AC up, dawg. It's hot as shit in here.

academentia

The state of being for a person in higher education in which they lose touch with all semblance of reality.

That professor used to be in touch with the profession, but now she suffers extreme academentia.

ACB

Short for "air-conditioner booty": a woman whose buttocks, when viewed from the side, resemble a wall-unit air conditioner protruding from a house.

Holly's ACB was knocking people's drinks off the table last night.

accountabilabuddy

A friend, maybe a best friend, who you get into trouble with and who is somewhat responsible for your actions.

Dude, Kyle is totally my accountabilabuddy. Good lookin' out, Kyle.

ADF

All day funk: What you smell like at the end of the day since your last shower.

I got to get home to take a shower. I have ADF.

ADHD

Attention deficit somethingk.

Hey! I spelled something wrong. Ha ha. Hey, look, a squirrel. Wait, what am I doing here again? Omigawd, my elbow itches. Wonder what's on TV? I like Jennifer Lopez. I hate kumquats. I really love urbandictionar . . . Where was I again? Hey! I don't have ADH . . . (Loses interest, chases after a bird.)

adorkable

Both dorky and adorable. A higher state of being all dorks strive toward.

That dork is so adorkable I could just hug him till I die.

advertainment

Media that advertises a product or brand while entertaining.

I love that Citroën advertisement with the giant dancing robot!

affluenza

Attempting to meet nonmaterial needs through the consumption of material goods.

My life sucks and I have no friends. . . . A trip to the mall will make me feel better!

afro puffs

A hairstyle in which the hair is tied into ball-shaped masses at the top or sides of the head. Typically found on those who have thick and somewhat frizzy hair.

Beyonce's rocking the afro puffs; she's cute as a button.

afterplay

The cuddling, kissing, etc., that occurs after sex.

Woman: The sex is great, but I wish there was more afterplay.

a-game

To do your best possible in any endeavor, not just in sports.

Y'all dudes better come wit it, I mean, bring ya a-game and shit.

AIMer

A person who talks so much on AIM that the terms of which transfer over to face-to-face conversations.

omg, lol that's so funny! Wait, g2g ttyl!

AIM rape

The act of messaging someone over and over against their will.

xXscottXx: Hey girl you wanna chat it up with me?

Girlie5: No

xXscottXx: Come on, lol, I haven't seen you since you got off the bus.

Girlie5: Shut up, stop talking to me.

xXscottXx: Shhh it's all good girl. just let it happen . . .

Girlie5: OMG! AIM rape! *block*

air

When someone gets blocked or ignored by somebody.

That girl gave him pure air.

air bags

Fake, silicone, saline, or otherwise augmented breasts.

Are those original equipment, or did she have air bags installed after market?

air biscuit

A fart or guff that is so potent it has a tangible quality. A butt burp that has a physical presence, and as such must be space made for it. Air biscuits may be launched, dropped, pushed out, chucked, etc.

Aw hell, I could pluck that air biscuit right out the air and dip it in my tea.

airborne coitus

Periphrastic speech for flying fuck, usually preceded by "I don't give a . . ."

I don't give an airborne coitus what Massachusetts senators think!

air hair

The thinning hair atop a balding man's head that you can see right through.

In the last seasons of his classic sitcom, Jerry Seinfeld's air hair became quite noticeable. So was Nicolas Cage's before he really went bald and had to wear a piece in his films.

air rage

Anger caused by poor service, bad food, cramped seats, or delays on an airplane.

After the plane sat on the tarmac for four hours, the flight attendants could do little to appease their passengers' air rage.

Alabama chrome

Duct tape.

Dude, you need to fix your car; some Alabama chrome will fix you up right.

alarmer

Someone who has a car alarm or a house alarm that has gone off accidentally. An alarmer who hasn't switched off their alarm is the worst kind.

Wonder when that alarm will stop going off like that. Oh, looks like it will be soon; I think that's the alarmer coming over.

alcohol abuse

Spilling alcohol, as in abusing it by wasting it.

You just spilled my beer all over the floor. That's alcohol abuse.

alcologic

Explanations given by a person who has been drinking and that only make sense to them.

Just ignore Louis. He is using alcologic again.

alcopops

Alcoholic soda pops. Modern-day drinks with fruity flavor, like lemon-ade or strawberry-flavored alcoholic drinks.

To attract a younger generation of drinkers, many liquor companies have created alcopops.

all

Another way of saying "said" or "says"; can be interchanged with "like" and "goes/go." Mostly used by teenage girls.

So she goes, "He's so fine," and I'm all "Hell, yeah!" and she's like "Damn," and I'm all "I know!"

all gravy
Good, fine.

It's all gravy.

all up in the Kool-Aid
A metaphor for saying that you're in our business.

Hillary and Jeanette are having a conversation when Sam starts to ask questions about what they're talking about.

"Dang," Hillary says. "All up in the Kool-Aid, and you don't even know the flavor!"

all up in your shit
To be in somebody's business.

Teachers are always all up in your shit.

alpha geek
The most knowledgeable, technically proficient person in an office or work group.

Hennings is the alpha geek of this corporation. He knows everything about the server.

ambisexual
A person with sexually ambiguous characteristics that don't define their gender. Guys who look like girls, girls who look like guys, and even someone with a name that can be used by both sexes.

Person 1: I have to meet someone called Sam.

Person 2: Sam? Is it a guy or a chick?

Person 1: Wow, I don't know. How ambisexual.

amish
To completely ground and deprive of all means of modern technology.

After my mom heard the truth about what happened last weekend, I was amished for weeks.

a.m. stripper
A low-grade exotic dancer, usually not the most attractive dancer in the establishment, who performs for the hungover, nontipping patrons during morning hours.

The burnt-out, stretch-marked alcoholic can barely afford her skanky clothes with the meager wages of her a.m. stripper job.

Ana
Short for anorexia nervosa, which is an eating disorder largely characterized by voluntary starvation and over-exercising.

When Sally feels really fat, she turns to Ana.

anablog
The old-fashioned journal you write in with crushed tree pulp, binding, and maybe some kind of lock mechanism. For some reason, people used to like writing opinions only they read. It is a fad past its prime but Borders still sells them.

Girl 1: What is that odd rectangular-shaped device you have in your lap that appears to be filled with blue-lined two-dimensional pieces of nondigital substance?

Girl 2: Oh, this is just my anablog. . . . I write in it to remember things and keep my private thoughts.

Girl 1: I see. So how do you post it when you're done?

the angles

Pics taken at different angles that form the illusion of beauty when in reality the subject of the picture is horribly disgusting looking.

Nick: I'm finally going to meet that girl I've been chattin' with online all year.

Mike: Oh, yeah? What's she look like?

(Nick shows Mike the pics.)

Mike: Oh, man, she has the angles!

The next day:

Nick: Holy shit, remember the girl I went to meet last night?

Mike: Yeah?

Nick: She was about five hundred pounds and bald. She looked like a Yeti. Oh yeah, her name was Kalis. Isn't a kalis something you get on the bottom of your foot?

angry ass

A burning sensation in the rectal area as a result of the consumption of large amounts of spicy foods.

Damn . . . those hot wings gave me angry ass.

angster

A term of endearment for one who is simultaneously defined as "emo" or "goth" and a "gangsta." A rare but potent combination.

Yo, Emil, stop bein' such a friggin' angster, yo!

animal beer

Different brands of cheap-ass beer with pictures of wild animals on their cans, e.g., Schmidt, Buckhorn, and Rhinelander.

All that animal beer last night gave me the beer shits.

anime hair

The geometry that occurs after one sleeps for six hours with hair that has either not been washed or had gel put in it before a person goes to sleep. Specifically, the polygons that form due to chronic stresses on the hair from a particular sleeping position.

Whoa, you've got some crazy anime hair going on.

anti

Unenthusiastic; against.

Geez! You're being so anti!

anysexual

One whose sexual preference is not

limited to man or woman or both. Targets include dinosaurs, rocks, fish, plankton, and balloons.

Chad is such an anysexual, he humped a penguin pillow last week.

AOL keyword

Used in a conversation to emphasize a point.

I don't think she knows yet.

AOL keyword: "Yet."

apartimony

Monies paid even though you are no longer living with a former roommate/lover.

I broke up with that skeezer Lisa and moved out. But I'm a good guy, so I'm still paying her apartimony.

apartment

A confined living space. A gerbil cage for humans. That is, a shower, microwave, food, bed, and toilet, all contained within a few hundred square feet. An apartment dweller typically knows the sex habits of the dweller above and the favorite music of the dweller next door, but would not recognize the face or name of either.

I just leased a new apartment. It's a nice unit; I don't have to wait long for the community clothes washer and it only costs 75 cents a load.

applejacked

The process of having your Apple iPod stolen, usually as a result of wearing the telltale white earbuds.

Person 1: Dude, I was on the train last night and someone came up to me and stole my iPod!

Person 2: Dude, you totally got applejacked.

approach anxiety

The butterflies feeling you get in your guts when you want to talk to an HB ("hot babe").

I've got a real sticking point with women. I can't get over my approach anxiety.

arm biter

It's the morning after a long night of drinking and carousing. You wake up with a crashing hangover, open your eyes, and discover the person you brought home to have sex with is frighteningly unattractive. And since your arm is trapped underneath that person, you would rather bite your arm off than wake them up.

That girl is an arm biter . . . coyote ugly.

arm candy

A remarkably attractive person of either sex accompanying you or some other lucky person.

Check out the arm candy with that dude!

around the way girl

The really cute/hot girl every neighborhood (usually urban) has and everyone wants to date/sleep with. There are usually rumors about this girl, since no one is actually brave enough to approach her . . . except LL Cool J. From LL Cool J's song "Around the Way Girl."

I want to do my hair, but I don't want to look too around the way girl, if you know what I'm sayin'.

artificially busy

Feeling like you have been extremely busy and you have no time for anything fun anymore, but never accomplishing anything.

Person 1: Man, I have been so busy but I just watched TV all day.

Person 2: Oh, that's just an artificially busy day.

artifishy

Almost like the real thing but not quite; usually said of foods, food colorings, food additives, etc.

This diner food sucks rope! The waiter says that these are homemade mashed potatoes, but they taste artifishy! I think the waiter's lying.

askhole

Someone who asks too many stupid, pointless, obnoxious questions.

God! Jimmy is such an askhole. He won't stop asking me about my favorite Teletubby and I'm about to smash him in the grill, kid.

askusation

A question and an accusation.

Are you flirting with my boyfriend?!

asparagus pee

The smelly urine that develops after eating fresh asparagus. It is said that everyone gets asparagus pee but only 20 percent of people can smell it. To those who can, the aroma is unmistakable, a uniquely bad smell. To those who can't, be careful to flush after eating a big plate of asparagus; you may make that new love interest run in terror.

Jen's asparagus pee was so rank that I had to go home and flush out my eyes. She didn't even seem to notice it! I don't think I can go there again.

assclown

A person who, while making a serious attempt at something, fails to realize what a complete fool he has made of himself.

The actor, while in character, made such an assclown of himself during the production that most of the audience started to talk during his monologues.

ass gasket

The toilet seat covers commonly found in public restrooms.

Ken left the stall with the ass gasket hanging out of his pants.

asshat

One whose head is so far up their rear end it could pass for a hat; used to describe a person who is stubborn, cruel, or otherwise unpleasant to be around.

Leave 'em alone, asshat!

assvice

The unwelcome and unsolicited advice given to someone.

Thanks for the assvice, but I think I'll do it my way.

astroturf

Creating the impression of public support by paying people in the public to pretend to be supportive. The false support can take the form of letters to the editor, postings on message boards in response to criticism, and writing to politicians in support of the cause. Astroturfing is the opposite of "grassroots," genuine public support of an issue.

Mike, admit you just got caught astroturfing. You're just pimping your own blog.

audible

To make an unexpected, last-minute decision. This definition is derived from its meaning in football.

Cara pulled an audible and called in sick to work.

Australian (or Aussie) kiss

Similar to a French kiss, but down under.

It started getting heavy when he started Australian kissing her.

automagically

Something that happens automatically, but that also has some mysterious, "magical" element to it. "Smart" appliances, features, etc., that do intelligent things with less help than you might expect.

I installed Windows, and it screwed up my system automagically!

avro

Aussie abbreviation of "afternoon."

I was gonna go buy some new dacks this avro, but mum a'ready bought me some!

awes

Abbreviation of the word awesome, cos shortening words is totally coo'.

Yo, that was so awes when you did that triple back flip.

awesinine

Stupidly brilliant or brilliantly stupid. Describes an idea or work whose chief virtue is its overwhelming, unadulterated dumbness.

dictionary

1 1

Person 1: Have you heard about that new movie Snakes on a Plane?

Person 2: Heck, yeah! I'm going opening night. That thing looks awesinine.

awesomeness test

An act of what appears to be generosity—such as lending an acquaintance a CD or movie, etc., or allowing them to choose what to do for fun—that is really more of a method of evaluating whether or not they're up to your cool standards.

When she let him pick which club to go to, he thought that she must really be into him, but in reality she was just giving him an awesomeness test.

a-whole-nother

Refers to a subject that is vastly or categorically set apart from the previous subject.

So we were all sitting there butt naked . . . but that's a-whole-nother story.

awkward arm

That arm that has nowhere to go when cuddling, spooning, or sleeping next to someone else. It usually leads to wishing arms could be pulled off and then put back on afterward.

After trying to settle into a comfortable spooning position: Uh-oh, it's the return of awkward arm!

awkward turtle

The animal mascot of the awkward moment. When you're in an awkward moment, place your hands on top of each other, then spin your thumbs forward, thus creating an awkward turtle.

Oh my God, so I was talking to Becky about STDs and I forgot she had syphilis. It was a mad awkward turtle.

AWKWARD TURTLE

The awkward turtle is better explained with a demonstration, and you can find many of them on YouTube. It's one of a set of gestures you can make to distract everyone from an awkward situation—and then make your hasty retreat. Other gestures include the "awkward antlers," the "awkward tent," and the "good story basket," all defined on urbandictionary.com.

B

A derivative of brother, which was, through usage, shortened to bro, and finally condensed to just B.

'Sup, B?

Get your ass over here, B.

Me and B are gonna book it downtown.

b/c

A word commonly used by teenagers while in instant messages or chatrooms. Short for "because."

Time for bed b/c tomorrow is gonna be a big day.

BA

Badass pronounced as bee-ay.

Your boyfriend is such a BA, yet he is so sweet to you.

babaloo

Has the same meaning as calling someone "sugarplum" or "sweetie." It's a slang version of "baby love" that with a lazy tongue turns into "babaloo."

Hi, Babaloo, how was your day?

babesicle

An extremely good-looking female usually with blond hair (although occasionally strawberry blond) and blue eyes. In certain rare cases, she may also have a unique and wildly attractive personality that could make an old man cry. Beauty and brains. Most male callers will find that they cannot keep up with a babesicle, as her fiery temper and lightning wit may be intimidating. Babesicles can be sexually dangerous for the unprepared! Better leave them to me.

Dude . . . she's a babesicle!

baby booking

Juvenile detention center.

You better have your toothbrush, son, because it's baby booking for you tonight.

baby leg

A large penis.

Humble Yet Happy Man: Girl, it's roughly about the size of a baby leg.

baby love

The opposite of platonic love between a man and a woman in which the two, in or out of a marital relationship, love each other in such a way that they both would consent to and enjoy conceiving a child together.

Oh, April and I? No no, sure I love her, but we don't have baby love!

babysit

To pay little or no attention to your alcoholic beverage, letting it sit idle, while you pretend to nurse it.

Hey, Nick, you getting paid to babysit that beer? Need a nipple?

back issue

1. Old news.

Yeah, she told me they broke up, but that's already back issue since it happened three weeks ago.

2. Something or someone that had its time, but has since faded from the scene.

The White Stripes? Nah, man, they're back issue now. Steriogram's where it's at now.

back-sass

Back talk, woffin', or talkin' trash.

Give me any more of that back-sass and I'll kick your ass.

backstalk

To go through an acquaintance's blog entries, even those dated before you met, in order to learn more about that person.

Sometimes I click the oldest link in Xanga to begin a backstalking session.

backyard

The posterior portion of the human body; substitutes for "bum," "butt," and "ass."

That man has a huge backyard; his tailor must be rich!

b'acne

Acne on your back.

Yay! It's b'acne day! And to think I was going to wear that lovely backless number. Polo neck it is then. I love summer.

bacon bit

A rent-a-cop; not good/important enough to be referred to as a pig or bacon, they're given the diminutive nickname of "bacon bit."

I thought we'd be in trouble when the 5-0 started rollin' up, but then I realized it was just the bacon bits they use for mall security.

bad for business

Anything that is not good for you, your life, or anything you do in life (aka "bad fo bidness").

Man, stay away from dat biatch, she bad for business. She gots the Hi 5.

badinkadink

A small, usually cute rear end on a female. As opposed to badonka-donk or badunkadunk, which is an extremely curvaceous female behind with moderately wide hips and a large amount of booty cleavage.

Damn, that girl's badinkadink ain't no comparison to my girl's badunkadunk!

bagged

A term used on the street to mean arrested.

Better wear a ski mask and gloves, I ain't trying to get bagged tonight.

bag hag

Gay man who accompanies rich women on shopping trips in order to be associated with fabulous shopping bags.

I totally have to get a bag hag—I'm tired of carrying my own Gucci shopping bags.

bagman

Someone who transports goods or money between people in a criminal activity. For example, a thug who comes around to collect extortion money and then takes it to a more senior gang member, or a lawyer who collects money to bribe a judge.

Give the money to the bagman and those speeding tickets will disappear.

bag of hammers

An insult referring to either the stupidity/low intelligence of another, or the uselessness of an idea, remark, or person.

When she opens her mouth, it sounds like someone just dropped a bag of hammers on a cold, concrete floor.

bag of pants

Useless. As would be a bag of pants, not fulfilling their function, but just hanging around in a bag.

Person 1: Sorry, we haven't got any.

Person 2: Well, that's just a bag of pants, isn't it.

bagsy

To claim something for yourself. There is no higher authority than a bagsy; once someone has bagsy'd something it can't be taken away. Compare "yoink."

I bagsy my seat. I gotta take a leak.

bagyanker

A male who constantly repositions his testicles.

He's such a bagyanker that when I first met him I was under the impression that he suffered from a medical condition in which his hand was conjoined with his balls.

bail out

To cheese it, as in run away, or get out of the way quickly.

I had to bail out of the exploding car.

bajangled

To be, or have been, intoxicated. Originally comes from "Mr. Bojangles."

Last night I was so bajangled, I passed out in the middle of the street.

bajiggity

When one person is hot for another.

Shenequa! Girl, you are so bajiggity for Daquawn.

bajillionaire

Someone with an insanely large sum of money.

Didja hear about Tedward? He just won the Megabowl. He's like totally a bajillionaire now!

bakeage

Drugs.

I need some bakeage.

baking brownies

When one farts excessively; the smell of "baking brownies."

Holy shit, Paul's baking brownies! Go to the toilet, Paul!

baleet

To delete something. Coined by Homestar Runner.

I baleeted my MySpace account today: MySpaceicide.

balla

1. A pimp.

I'm a balla fo' real.

2. Someone who is good at sports.

Allen Iverson is a balla.

ball drain

A person who always kills the mood, is often whiny and negative, and whose attitude is so draining that it puts you in a foul mood.

I hate hanging out with Karen. She is such a ball drain.

baller block

When someone baller blocks you they are hindering your attempt to get your mack on with a member of the opposite sex. This heinous crime is punishable by castration, Chinese water torture, slow painful death, or community service.

Todd: Man, last night was a bitch. I was

trying to work my game on that hot chick from the PR department, but some asshole was hanging all over her the entire night. Total baller block.

Luke: That was her husband, dude.

Todd: Still . . .

ballhammer

A major annoyance. A situation that causes dread in one's life.

Damn, waking up to my clock radio playing that Don Henley cover by the Ataris was such the ballhammer.

ballin'

Extremely rich and likes to show it off.

Master P is ballin' with all his money.

balloonjuice

1. Insincere or empty talk, nonsense.

Can the balloonjuice and get back to work.

2. Interjection meaning "Nonsense!"

You bought a new Porsche for $50? Balloonjuice!

ball out

To leave.

I'm bouts to ball out of this joint.

balls 'n' all

A passionate expression for saying "everything"; the works.

I'll have a supersize combo, balls 'n' all!

balltickler

Someone who exhibits homosexual tendencies in an aggressive way.

After I nailed the last guy to win our dodgeball game, the whole team gave me high fives, except for Steve, who smacked me in the ass. What a balltickler that guy is.

baltic

Very, very cold.

It was baltic out there. I don't want to end up getting frostbite.

Baltimore love

In a 50 Cent song he refers to Baltimore love as the relationship between an addict and heroin. Baltimore love is the addiction that heroin addicts feel.

Damn, dude, I've got so much Baltimore love I could just die.

bam

Scottish colloquial. Means below-average mentality.

Ah'm nae a bam, like!

bambina

Italian for "little girl," used as slang for a good-looking young woman. Used like "baby" in English.

To a pretty girl walking down the street: Hey, bambina, you break-a my heart! Where you going? Come with me!

bamboo

Rolling papers and/or Zig-Zags.

Let me get some bamboo to roll this up with.

BAMF

Badass motherfucker.

Wow, that Dane Cook is one BAMF.

bammer

1. Lacking in quality, usually pertaining to weed or other street drugs.

Don't gimme no bammer weed—we don't smoke no shit in the SFC.

2. Qualitatively negative; bad; lame; shitty.

This shit is hella bammer.

About fifty million people visited urbandictionary.com in 2006, and two out of three people were from the United States. Other countries with a lot of Urban Dictionary visitors are the United Kingdom, Canada, Australia, Germany, Netherlands, France, Sweden, Poland, India, and Italy.

DEFINE YOUR WORLD

banana basket

Underwear, as they are used to store a man's banana.

Dude, you just popped out of your banana basket.

banana clip

A large-capacity magazine for automatic weapons, named "banana clip" because its shape resembles a banana.

Yo, Mannie, pass me that banana clip so I can load this AK.

banana head

An insulting term for someone who is mentally challenged.

Quit drooling on yourself, banana head.

banana problem

Not knowing when enough is enough. From the story of the kid who said, "I know how to spell 'banana,' I just don't know when to stop."

The totally unnecessary twenty-three cup holders in my mom's SUV are an example of a banana problem.

bananus

The little brown part at the bottom of a banana that no one in their right mind eats.

Only monkeys eat the bananus.

bananza

To act crazy; dance crazily; dance like nobody is around.

Oh my god, Becky is going bananza.

ban cannon

Banning someone from an Internet message board.

I had to place a ban cannon on an idiot because he wouldn't stop breaking the forum guidelines.

B & BJ

A seedy hotel; the kind of place that may even rent rooms by the hour; a place you go solely for sex.

She's totally hot! I took her to that B & BJ over on Forty-Second.

band candy

Sex that band members get from groupies.

Man, I totally scored some band candy last night—that chick was hot.

B&M

Brick and mortar. The physical location of a business, as opposed to its online location.

This purchase is not available online, only B&M.

bandwidth

Ability to complete work given the available resources (people, time, money, etc.).

Since we can't afford to replace the guy who just quit, our department doesn't have enough bandwidth to take on new projects right now.

bang

To be a gangster.

Ey, foo, you bang?

bangable

Worthy of your sexual attention and pleasure, whether it be a male or female.

Lisa: Emo boys are very much bangable.

Meghan: I agree. Their cute little man purses and artificial sadness really turn me on.

bang a left

Slang typically heard in Boston. It is not just making a left turn, it is to make a left as soon as the light goes green and before the oncoming traffic has a chance to react to the light changing to green.

I can't believe that there's no green arrow at this busy intersection. It looks like I'll have to bang a left if I ever want to get through it.

bangbangbang

To have raw, dirty, demeaning sex. Made famous by the Arabian rap artists Gröûp X in their song "I Just Want (Bang, Bang, Bang)."

My ex just wants bangbangbang every time I see her.

bang dat

Hell, yeah. An expression of general agreement or satisfaction, with gusto.

Person 1: Smoke another?

Person 2: Bang dat!

banging the queen

Hooking up with a person solely for the story. References Queen Elizabeth II of England. No rational man (or lesbian) would want to have sexual intercourse with this woman, but upon learning that she is the queen of England, she becomes instantly worth sleeping with. Why? Because you could tell people who you just banged. Can be applied by women as well (porking the prince).

Guy 1: Dude, wouldn't it be awesome to hook up with Britney Spears?

Guy 2: Gross, man. She's all fat and nasty now.

Guy 1: But it'd be worth it. You'd totally be banging the queen if you did.

bang my hammer

A subtle way of saying "You turn me on" or "You float my boat." It can also be used in a nonsexual way to describe something that one likes.

Tay, you bang my hammer.

bang out

To stomp someone out or beat them badly.

I hate that kid. I'm gonna bang him out!

bangover

The aching feeling you have after a night of rough sex, sometimes creating the need to take Advil.

The guy I hooked up with up last night gave me a wicked bangover.

bang piece

1. Something you consider totally awesome.

Wow, this new video game is my bang piece!

2. Someone you have casual sex with but have absolutely no respect for.

Pamela? She's nothin' but a bang piece.

bang up

To intravenously inject something.

I love spinach so much I'm gonna get some and bang it up.

banjaxed

Broken, ruined; can also mean tired.

Jaysus, after that lifting them bricks all day I'm bleedin' banjaxed.

banked

Baltimore term for when one person is assaulted or beat up by multiple persons.

They banked me for my chain when I got off from work.

bankles

Boobs that sag all the way down to your ankles.

Dude, that chick has bankles!

bap

Black American princess.

Shauna is a mover and shaker who knows that Mikimoto provides pearls and Burberry is not sold in the flea market. Total bap!

bar

1. British slang for money. One bar equals one pound.

It's five bar to get into the club.

2. A 2 mg Xanax tablet. Derived from its long, barlike shape.

Florida governor Jeb Bush's daughter was arrested for calling in a bullshit prescription for Xanax bars.

barage

A residential garage that has been converted to look like a public bar.

G-Man spent some time in a barage on Veterans Day twisting off.

Barbara Feldon

In poker, a pair of nines. Barbara Feldon's character on the TV show *Get Smart* was known only as "Ninety-Nine."

You've got a pair of eights, but I've got Barbara Feldon!

barberphobe

Derogatory term for a male who has very long hair. Derived from the notion that such people don't cut their hair because they're afraid of barbers.

That boy in French class has a ponytail. What a barberphobe!

Barbie moment

Being completely stupid; acting like a fool; not remembering something.

One plus one equals three . . . oops! I had a Barbie moment!

bardcore

A pornographic movie with a Shakespearean plot.

Dude, I just saw my first bardcore movie, A Midsummer's Night Cream!

bare back

To have sex without using a condom.

I couldn't find any condoms, so we went bare back.

barfarrhea

Diarrhea while vomiting. Barfarrhea is often caused by food poisoning.

It was the worst case of barfarrhea I've ever had.

bargument

A confrontation, physical or verbal, stemming from or taking place at an establishment that serves alcohol.

The drunk guy started a bargument with the bouncer and got dropped in the alley.

bark eater

A person who is one with nature. Tree hugger.

She's a bark eater, so she doesn't spend much money on makeup and toiletries.

barking at the ants

Vomiting, especially in the street.

Landlord: You look rough, mate.

Gus: I know, I've been barking at the ants all evening. I think it's your dodgy beer.

Landlord: Well, you did drink nineteen pints.

barma

Drinkers' karma.

A good tip equals good barma. A bad tip equals bad barma.

barn

Short for barnacle. One who latches onto someone superior to them (the hull).

Hi, my name's Johnny, and these are Richard and Douglas, my two barns.

barsexual

A college-age girl who kisses other girls in bars and clubs, usually for attention and the approval of men.

A bisexual girl kisses girls at home when no one's looking. A barsexual girl kisses them only in places that charge a cover.

bar star

A guy or girl who goes to clubs or bars at least once a week. Usually bar stars are found at clubs every Friday and Saturday night.

Person 1: I never see Joe on the weekends; where is he?

Person 2: He's a bar star, so he's clubbing.

bar steward

A way of getting away with calling someone a bastard in polite company, like in front of your mom.

He's a complete bar steward!

bartard

One who acts like a 'tard at a bar.

Jeff got really drunk at the Hurricane on Saturday and started dancing like a bartard.

base head

A crack addict.

Man, that guy smokes so much rock. What a base head.

bashment

A West Indian party where reggae music is played excessively. Rap music is also thrown in the DJ's mix, but the music is heavily dominated by reggae. A party where you're most likely to see the latest dances and some of the sexiest West Indian women wearing almost nothing. Flatbush, Brooklyn, is known to throw some of the craziest bashments in NYC.

Yo, there's a bashment in Flatbush tonight, son.

basshole

A jackass who drives through residential areas at three in the morning with the subwoofers on his car stereo at maximum volume.

I was enjoying a restful slumber when this basshole came driving by, causing everything in my apartment to rattle as if hit by an earthquake.

basskitten

A modern-times female with sex appeal; generally associated with the techno music scene.

I went to this rave over the weekend and hooked up with this hot basskitten.

bat cave

The place where you hide your porn from your wife/girlfriend.

Person 1: Dude, where's your booby mags?

Person 2: In my bat cave.

batcaving

Asocial suburban behavior in which people enter and exit their house by way of the garage, avoiding social

interaction with neighbors, passers-by, and the outside world. The key to effective batcaving is the automatic garage door opener. Gated communities provide high opportunities for batcavability.

Person 1: Did you hear about that woman in the news? She lives around here!

Person 2: How would anyone know? Out here, neighbors go batcaving in and out of their place and we never see them. Except when they mow the lawn. And everybody pays to have that done anyway.

bath dodger

A person who bathes only once a week; aka "soap dodger."

Geez, the smell of that bath dodger would rot the nose hairs off a dead wombat.

bat-shit

Extremely; very; to a degree beyond normal reckoning.

She's bat-shit insane.

battle

To rap orally against another individual, as in a contest; to orally recite rap or hip-hop lyrics back and forth between two or more individuals.

Jay Kay and I were in a battle together against Jaime's group.

battle rims

Most cheap cars come stock with "battle rims." When you take the hubcap off of the wheel, you'll find a battle rim underneath. Battle rims are the stock, ugly-looking, cheapest type of wheels on earth. They will get you from A to B, or you can take your car to a destruction derby with these wheels.

While driving through the ghetto, I noticed a crackhead driving a caddy that had two spare tires on one side and two battle rims on the other side. I said to myself, "WTF?"

Bauer

To seriously wreck someone's flow, especially in the style of Jack Bauer.

Darryl was having a nice day, but I had to Bauer his ass when he talked to my girl.

bow chika bow wow

The sound of a '70s porn riff.

We didn't rent last night; we made our own videos. Bow chicka bow wow.

ba-zing

Used at the end of a sentence in which someone said something witty or even a joke; can be heard on the cartoon show *Family Guy*.

Person 1: Man, this shit is tight!

Person 2: That's what your momma told me last night, ba-zing!

bazza

A barrel; a barreling wave formation. Slang used most often by surfers.

I pulled into a massive bazza.

BB

Bye-bye.

BB, cya!

BBML

Be back much later.
Used when you won't be back for a very long time.

I got to go to Florida. BBML

BDSM

An overlapping abbreviation of bondage and discipline (BD), dominance and submission (DS), and sadism and masochism (SM).

Are you actually into BDSM or do you just carry that leather whip for show?

beached

So unresponsive that one resembles a beached whale. Often due to excessive intake of alcohol or marijuana. Hammered, blitzed.

I got messed up pretty bad last night. I was just laying on my buddy's couch staring at the people walking by. I guess you could say I was beached.

beach-slap

To be knocked down by a large wave. Implies losing something of value in the ocean.

Man, I was bodysurfing last week and lost my glasses when I got beach-slapped by a twenty-footer.

beak

1. To make fun of.

Dude, are you mad cuz I was beakin' you, eh?

2. Cocaine.

Got any more o dat beak there, lad?

bear

A term used by gay men to describe a husky, large man with a lot of body hair.

George's sexual tastes run toward bears.

bear bait

On a highway, a car that passes you going way over the posted speed limit. If there is a speed trap ahead, he will get caught instead of you. Also called a "cop cleaner."

Trucker 1: Breaker, breaker. Jimmy, I gotta make up some time. Any bears around? Over.

Trucker 2: Not seen any, Peter. But that young buck that blew by us in the Eclipse musta been doing about ninety. Bear bait fer sure. Over.

beardo

A weirdo with a beard.

In my travels I am constantly on the lookout for strange new beardos.

beast it

To use brute strength and massive force to do something; going crazy on an object.

Person 1: Stupid stapler. It's not working.

Football player: Just beast it.

Person 1: Wow, cool, it works now.

beastly

When you're totally friggin' awesome at something.

Dude, you're so beastly at scaring little kids by posing as Michael Jackson.

beastmaster

A woman who is heinous.

The girl is a beastmaster.

beast mode

1. A state of serious training or a level of high effort.

Animal was going beast mode at practice.

2. An energetic, outgoing state of mind.

Whenever I hit the bar, my mind goes into beast mode.

beat

1. To have sex.

Yo dogg, we beat last night.

2. Lame.

Man, this party is beat!

beatbox

To use your mouth to create the

sounds of a drum set. Often used as an accompaniment to freestyling or flowing.

To get the little campers to go to sleep, Erik and Manuel beatboxed while Jacob busted out with mad rhymes.

beat cheeks

To leave the area quickly. Originally from the fact that each lobe of your buttock will be slapping together during the act of running.

C'mon, man, the cops will be here any minute. Let's beat cheeks!

beating

A chick who has a high maintenance/ better-than-you attitude and acts like you aren't worth her time; a chick who nags and is controlling in a relationship.

Dude, that chick is such a beating. She won't let John come to the movies with us because she thinks he'll go pickin' up on other girls.

beat off

Masturbate; jack off.

Been beatin' off like a madman lately.

beaucoup

A lot; many; a remarkable amount.

They had beaucoup people at the car wash Saturday.

beautality

The raw, indescribable quality of something that is at once beautiful and painful; beautiful and brutal combined.

While filled with a glorious beauty seldom seen on this earth, her honesty made her a dangerous foe. She truly exemplified beautality.

beautimous

Used to describe a situation, thing, or person that is extremely positive.

Person 1: I'm going to a Playboy *shoot in Hawaii for spring break!*

Person 2: Beautimous, man!

be easy

Calm yo nerves; chill out; stay cool.

Man, if I have to tell you one mo time, be easy, fo' we get caught.

beer bitch

The person designated to get the beer from the refrigerator or cooler.

We had never seen this guy before, so we made him our beer bitch.

beer cataracts

An extreme variant of the condition *beer goggles*, where massive alcohol consumption leads to a male completely losing his ability to sense female repugnancy.

Guy 1: Did you see that rotter that Mark was talking to? Nasty case of beer goggles there.

Guy 2: More like beer cataracts. She had a beard growing out of her ass.

beer emergency

The condition in which no more beer is present for consumption.

Dude, we've got a beer emergency! We need to go on a beer run immediately.

beer trophy

When you wake up in the morning after a night out and find a traffic cone/for sale sign/gnome, etc., in your room, you have a beer trophy. Beer trophies are distributed by the beer fairy for good drinking efforts.

I woke up and found a shopping cart in the front room—biggest beer trophy I ever got.

beeshee

Shortened form of the word "bull-shit"; often used in place of any and every expletive.

Shut the beeshee up, you beeshee!

beezy

Word used instead of the word "bitch."

That girl's a punk-rock beezy.

belly bling

Navel rings or any other bling for the belly button.

It was the first warm day of a brand new spring,

The chicks were all out showing off their belly bling.

belly fire

A burning feeling deep in the stomach, usually caused by spicy food, Bloody Marys, or just drinking in general.

After that plate of wings and a couple spicy Bloody Marys, I had some serious belly fire.

belly scrapenz

Any food that falls and hangs onto or stains one's shirt, tie, or coat, which is later consumed by the offender or a pet.

Mr. Jones snarfed some belly scrapenz off his tie.

belly washer

A carbonated beverage or soda.

Man, I could use a ice-cold belly washer today.

bending corners in the hood

Walking around your neighborhood looking for things to do.

I was hanging with my homies bending corners in the hood.

bengal

A chick with an ugly face but a smoking body; also called a "brown-bagger." After the football team Cincinnati Bengals, who have sweet jerseys but terrible helmets.

That chick looked great from behind, but she turned out to be a total bengal.

bent

1. To be dishonest or corrupt; often used in reference to a police officer.

Supt. Tucker was a bent cop.

2. To be severely intoxicated by narcotics and/or alcohol.

Yeah, I don't remember anything from last night; I was bent as hell.

3. To be homosexual or effeminate in appearance or nature.

You are so friggin' bent!

bergina

What a fake gynecologist calls a vagina.

OK, Meg, let's take a look at that bergina.

besties

Friends who are always there for each other, no matter what. Closer than a best friend, because best friends fight sometimes and besties don't.

Me and Jill are totes besties.

bia

Term of endearment, usually to a good friend. Slang for "bitch"; short for "biatch."

What's up, bia?

biatchitude

Displaying behavior and attitude typical of a biatch.

What's with the biatchitude? You got a problem?

bibble

Freshy fresh; fly; dope; boo-tey-licious.

Well shizzle my nizzle, Gridley's van is so way bibble.

bid

A prison sentence.

My man is doing a bid in Rikers for attempted murder.

biddie

An attractive, available girl. It is a subjective word, so a girl can be a biddie to one person and not to another. A girl who is just friends with a guy cannot be considered his biddie. Girls with boyfriends cannot be biddies.

Damn, I'm gonna meet some biddies tonight.

biddie bounce

A way of walking to impress all of the biddies.

Ay yo, let's biddie bounce out of here so we can find some bitches.

bidness

The opposite of legitimate business; A street hustle, or a shady and mostly illegal business venture; dealings that aren't exactly "street legal."

Bloomingdale's = business. Selling dresses and purses out of your trunk = bidness.

BIF

Acronym for "butt in front." Usually associated with middle-aged to elderly women in stretchy polyester pants which, when pulled up high enough, give the illusion of their ass actually being in the front.

Dude, my old aunt's got a BIF so big, she can rest a Pepsi bottle on it.

bifta

A reefa, a spliff, a joint; i.e., a marijuana roll.

Pass the bifta.

big-boned

A nice way of saying one is fat, built in an odd way, or a giant.

Person 1: Am I fat, Mommy?

Person 2: No, of course not, sweetie. You're just big-boned.

Big Dog

President Bill Clinton.

Big Dog still has mucho mojo in political circles.

bimmer

A BMW automobile. Also "beemer."

The M5 is the ultimate bimmer.

bing

Prison or jail.

Cousin Ray's out the bing.

binger

A full chamber of marijuana smoke inhaled from a bong. The act of ripping a binger is widely practiced.

Bill rips mad bingers.

bio-accessory

A living being used as a fashion accessory, like a handbag or a scarf, except that it's alive; often dressed up in cutesy little outfits.

Paris Hilton rarely goes out without her bio-accessory, Tinkerbell the Chihuahua. Britney Spears used to carry around her bio-accessory, Bit Bit, until she started carrying around babies instead.

bio break

Neo-geek terminology for visiting the bathroom, especially when interrupting a meeting/gathering/workflow.

Person 1: Where's Jones? I need him in here now!

Person 2: Oh, he's on bio break, but I'll send him right in.

bio-chocolate

Feces, shit, poo; short for "biological chocolate."

Someone just dropped the illest bio-chocolate in there.

biodome

The type of large, nonflat, see-through plastic lid used to cover Slurpees and various iced coffee drinks that allows for wide spillover of whipped cream and other edible, nonliquid material.

Oh, no! My straw's too short for the biodome. . . . I'm losin' it!

biPodding

Sharing a single set of headphones attached to one iPod. One person holds the iPod and takes the left earbud; the other takes the right earbud. Can be performed while moving.

They biPodded down the street; Jane had the left earpiece, Sarah the right.

birthmas gift

The double gift for a person unfortunate enough to be born on or around Christmas.

I was born on December 23 and never get separate birthday and x-mas gifts. I always get some lame birthmas gift. Thanks a lot, Santa!

bis cas fri

This is how we say business casual Friday around the office, because, you know, we have to abbrev everything.

I'm going to wear my Win XP polo shirt this bis cas fri.

bisexy

Appealing to both sexes.

Your boyfriend isn't gay but thinks Brad Pitt is hot because Brad is bisexy.

bish

A shortened version of the word "bitch." Commonly used when it is inappropriate to swear; mostly used as an insult.

English teacher: Did you get your home-work done last night?

Student: No.

English teacher: Why not?

Student: Because you're a bish.

bit

Simple insult that pertains to any-one. Similar to "asshole" or "bitch."

That little bit stole my steely and drank it while I was bangin' that hottie.

bitchless

Single man.

John went to the New Year's Eve party bitchless.

bitch move

A decision that can be classified as weak or cowardly.

Punching that guy in his sleep was a bitch move.

bitch tits

Male breasts; man boobs.

Bob has bitch tits. Damn, that chubber gotta get himself fitted for a bra.

biter

Copier, follower.

She is such a biter—she totally copied my outfit.

bitgod

Acronym for "back in the good old days"; someone who yearns for the way things used to be.

Flintstone was a real bitgod about pop music; having been a teen during the '80s, she thought everything that came after Duran Duran was crap.

b'jesus

Small spirit that lives inside all living things. In times of extreme emotion, it leaves the body. More than "good god" and "Jesus Christ," b'jesus expresses a crazy amount of shock. Also spelled "bajeezus" or "ba-jesus."

Holy crap, you scared the b'jesus outta me!

black Friday

The day after Thanksgiving in the U.S. It's traditionally the busiest shopping day of the year (and sometimes considered to be the beginning of the Christmas season); aka "Green Friday."

I'm holding out on buying my Christmas gifts this year until black Friday rolls around, so I can get the best deals.

bladder buster

Any of the ubiquitous, huge, outrageously obnoxious soft drink containers sold in convenience stores. The bladder buster has gotten so large that no vehicle's cup holder can hold it. When you urinate after drinking one, the fire department's hazmat team is summoned and the EPA files an incident report.

Damn, Frank filled his bladder buster at the truck stop and then we had to stop every twenty minutes so he could squirt the dirt.

blag

To gain entrance to a restricted area or club or some material good through confident trickery or cheekiness; lying is also acceptable.

I blagged my way into the VIP area and then blagged some free CDs off the label.

blended

Able to go unnoticed in a situation or crowd.

Mickey always acts blended when we go out because the only color he rocks is black.

blind item

When a gossip columnist doesn't have enough evidence to support a claim about a celebrity and gives mild clues to the identity instead of names.

Today's blind item: Which blonde is no longer giving sweet kisses to her boy-band husband?

blinkered

Not open to other ideas; single-minded. Horses wear blinkers that keep them from getting startled by movement in their peripheral vision.

People who buy iPods are so blinkered.

blinker fluid

An imaginary liquid used in automobiles to make the blinkers work. This term is used as a sarcastic remark toward someone who knows absolutely nothing about cars.

Bob: My car's broken again. I don't know what's wrong.

Jon: Did you check the blinker fluid?

blipster

A black hipster, in appearance, musical taste, and social scene. Popularized by the *New York Times* in January 2007.

I'm a blipster wearing Asics Tigers and black-rimmed glasses. I rock to the new Be Your Own Pet song.

blockormore

A girl who only looks good from a block or more away. Similar to "butterface."

Dag, that girl is ugly. She's definitely a blockormore.

blog fodder

An interesting idea, story, or link. Referred to as blog fodder when your first reaction is to use it in your blog.

I'm sorry your day sucked, but between the car wreck, the kiss-off, and the layoff, at least you've got some real blog fodder.

blogorrhea

To write a blog entry just for the sake of posting an entry, not because you have done anything interesting today.

I couldn't really think of anything good to blog about, so my last post was real blogorrhea.

blogsmack

Using a blog to broadcast something slanderous, disrespectful, scandalous, or embarrassing about someone.

The president was blogsmacked around the Internet today, with left-wing bloggers having a field day with his latest antics in the Oval Office.

blogspeak

A language developed for and used

in Internet journals, or blogs, by their keepers, or bloggers.

A meme is blogspeak for an idea spread from blog to blog.

blondourage
An entourage of attractive, scantily clad young blond women who accompany a high-profile male celebrity to public events.

Hugh Hefner is amazing. I saw him out last night with seven blond bunnies. He's got quite a blondourage.

blow a smoke ring
To overheat or overload electronic equipment, causing damage to the overheated component and associated system failure.

I'm not sure yet, but it looks like a fan went south and the processor gagged. I hope it didn't blow a smoke ring.

blue angel
The ignition of one's flatulence; usually achieved by holding a lighter near the anus while passing gas. The term comes from the bluish-colored flame often resulting from methane combustion.

I have always enjoyed doing blue angels but decided to discontinue the activity the day that a flame singed my lower intestines.

bluebird
Cop, police officer, security guard, etc.

There's a bluebird on my shoulder.

bluetool
A person who wears a Bluetooth wireless earpiece everywhere they go to seem trendy and important. Places to spot bluetools include movie theaters, malls, restaurants, gyms, grocery stores, and in cars.

Bluetool: Hey, how are you?

Megan: I'm great, and yourself?

Bluetool: Oh, sorry, Megan. I wasn't talking to you, I'm on a call. Bluetooth.

BLUETOOL

"Bluetool" resonated with many readers when it became word of the day on May 10, 2007—thousands of people agreed with Urban Dictionary's description of the curious fashion statement.

ud

bluewalls
The female equivalent of blueballs.

Andre gave Christina bluewalls . . . and then he drove to Taco Bell to eat a grande meal.

B Minus
Bud Light.

Hey, Rick, Sally called and wants us to pick up some B Minus and vodka and come over to play Kings.

BNIB

Brand new in box. Often used in auctions and sales, particularly online.

Auction title: "Adidas Superstars. Men's size 11 U.S. BNIB"

boat

A full house in poker.

Person 1: Ace high flush! Pay up, bitch!

Person 2: Not so fast! I've got the boat.

Person 1: Damn!

boat casual

A dressed-down preppy who is still wearing fancy clothes, as if they were going out in their boat, and were scared that the surf would be rough and get them all wet, so they wore Top-Siders, khaki shorts, and a T-shirt from a 10K race from eight years ago.

His dad was kickin' it boat casual on the back deck by the grill, getting barbecue sauce on that old pair of Dockers shorts that he wears whenever he does yard work.

Bob

Battery-operated boyfriend (vibrator).

I need a man, but I'll settle for Bob!

bodge

A quick and dirty job; something done very hastily. Make it look good for the next day or two and if it falls down after that, it's all right.

Person 1: You bodged together that doghouse, didn't you?

Person 2: How can you tell?

Person 1: The walls look like they could cave in at any time.

bo-duke it

To enter a vehicle such as a convertible or Jeep by jumping in the side rather than opening the door.

I had to bo-duke it while running from the cops.

body spam

Unsolicited physical contact.

Dude, Aunt Lynn totally just body spammed me with that hug!

bog

A toilet.

I need to go to the bog.

boho

Bohemian; very hip, but not exactly trendy; often creative or artsy; having a unique sense in fashion.

Ugh, those Converses are so not boho. Can anybody say conformist?

boif

Boyfriend; male you are dating.

Me and the boif are going to the movies later, want to come?

bolt-ons

Breast augmentation; boob job.

Krissy's dad paid for her new bolt-ons.

Bonaparte

Nickname for one who is short in stature and tends to overcompensate for it, often through a short temper, learning martial arts or other fighting skills, or attempting excessively difficult tasks.

Short dude: What are you lookin' at? You wanna start something?

Tall dude: Whoa, Bonaparte, mellow out.

Bond Year

A year that ends in 007, such as 2007.

Countdown to 2007: 3, 2, 1, Happy Bond Year!

bonely

Bored and lonely.

Me: Mommy, I'm feeling so bonely!!!

Mommy: Oh, honey, don't be sad. I know what will make you feel better. I made your most favorite food.

Me: Really, what?

Mommy: Roti and dahl!

Me: Yay! I don't feel bonely anymore!

bones

Dollars.

He owes me fifty bones.

bong flu

One of any number of contagious diseases transmitted through the use of marijuana paraphernalia.

David entered the rotation with a cold, and now we've all got bong flu.

bonus beer

Beer that one "discovers," having not known that it was there. Typically this occurs after a party or family gathering/event and may often involve a secondary fridge or forgotten cooler. Discovery of said beer is usually followed by feelings of joy and well-being, similar to finding unexpected money in a jacket one has not worn in some time.

I'll just clean out the fridge; haven't done that in a while. Wait a sec, what's this? Bonus beer! Righteous!

boo

Boyfriend or girlfriend.

Are you playing me? If you are, you ain't gonna be my boo.

boob assisted

To have unfairly achieved something purely through the possession of large breasts and despite a lack of relevant knowledge or skills.

Jenny got the last bagel just by sticking her breasts out.

boof

Goofy, messed up, or otherwise out of the ordinary.

I boofed my 9-iron and hit my foot instead of the ball.

booger sugar

Cocaine.

I went to my dealer to get some booger sugar.

boomin'

Slammin', fly, superfine, unfathomably hot, and oh-so-delicious. Irresistible—not that you would try to resist.

Did you see Matt this morning? Damn, if that ass didn't look boomin'!

booming

On psychedelic mushrooms.

Colten is booming this weekend; he got a quarter of some bomb-ass shrooms.

booty chatter/chatta

Talkin' stuff; talkin' trash. Unnecessary gossip about someone or something.

He ain't talkin' nothin' but booty chatta.

booty cutters

Very small shorts on a very shapely, large butt.

Dang, I know it's hot out here, but those booty cutters she's wear'n is killin' me.

booty do

When a girl's stomach sticks out farther than her booty do.

Do you think I have booty do?

booty poppin'

When a girl shakes her ass without moving her body.

I think I lost a few pounds last night. There was some intense booty poppin' goin' down.

borange

Any object, theme, or concept of extremely poor quality. Rubbish.

That shirt is borange.

boredid

Really really really bored.

I'm boredid cuz I can't talk to my baby right now.

born-again virgin

A formerly promiscuous person's commitment to not have sex again until marriage.

After Mike had been sleeping with Sara for a year and she left him for the well-endowed circus midget, he decided it was time to become a born-again virgin.

boss up

To step your game up; get on the next level.

Boy, boss up and get this money!

bottom drawer

To be asked to work overtime for free, or otherwise be taken advantage of by an employer.

I got so bottom drawered today!

box lock

The female equivalent of a cock block.

I was hitting on that guy, but my girlfriend stepped in and totally box locked me.

bracketology

The art and science of figuring out NCAA basketball tournament brackets during March Madness.

Hmm . . . Well, don't put any teams from Pac 10 to pass second round on your bracket this year. I'm serious.

brain candy

An experience that is enjoyable because it stimulates the mind pleasantly but doesn't actually make it work. Usually in reference to light and fluffy books, movies, TV shows, and other entertainment. Akin to eye candy.

No one ever called Star Trek *great drama, but it makes pretty good brain candy.*

brain cramp

A stupid, and perhaps embarrassing, mistake.

I had a brain cramp and for a moment couldn't remember which hand was my right.

brain glue

When it feels as though bits of your brain have been disconnected (i.e., when you're feeling stupid), this substance helps to stick them back together again. Sadly, it has not yet been invented.

I went out partying all night and was in serious need of some brain glue the next morning!

brain grenade

A bottle of beer, due to its effect on brains.

The game's about to start. Toss me a brain grenade, Jack.

brand whore

Someone who buys and prominently displays name-brand products (or products that feature large corporate logos) under the belief that such loyalty to a label or corporation brings prestige to their otherwise lack of taste, regardless of the actual quality or value of the products; aka "label whore," "brand slave."

That kid is wearing a Nike jacket, Nike shorts, and Nike shoes—do you think Nike is paying this brand whore to wear all of their apparel?

Brangelina

The relationship of Brad Pitt and Angelina Jolie.

Aah, I am so sick of hearing about Brangelina in the tabloids!

break the glass

To break out the big guns. Resorting to your emergency plan when everything you've tried has failed. From breaking the glass of fire extinguishers to put out a fire.

There's nothing to do. It's time to break the glass and go to urbandictionary.com.

break your crayons

Make you very upset or sad, or ruin your whole day.

Dude, don't worry about him, he's just tryin' to break your crayons. Just let it slide.

breezin'

Hanging out; chilling.

Jeyanna: Hey, girl, what are you up to tonight?

You: Oh, not too much. Just breezin' with some homies.

bridge and tunnel

Term used by Manhattan elitists for people who venture into "The City" who have to travel via bridge or tunnel to arrive, specifically those people from New Jersey or Long Island. Traditionally, people who live in Brooklyn, the Bronx, and even Staten Island are exempt from this term. This is not a favorable term, and at times is synonymous with "trash."

The Gotti kids are bridge and tunnel to the core: They have stupidly lavish parties here that real New Yorkers would never have,

and they use too much gel.

briefcake

A handsome male lawyer.

Did you check out the briefcake in courtroom C?

brill

British slang for "brilliant," equivalent of American "cool."

That was bloody brill!

bring a book

Boring.

No hitting, alcoholism, or passive-aggressive behavior between you two? You call that a relationship? Bring a book!

bring it back

To tell the DJ to "bring that song back." In other words, to request an encore.

DJ, bring it back!

bring it, don't sing it

An expression intended to inspire an individual to take action on a certain subject as opposed to constantly talking about said subject.

Drunk 1: I am gonna drink more tonight than you ever could. I bet you $1,000 I can bong three cases of beer and slam thirty shots!

Drunk 2: The night is young. . . . Come on and bring it, don't sing it.

bring your own sand to the beach

Taking your girlfriend/boyfriend to a party or social event where there will be plenty of single women/men to mingle with.

Damn, can you believe that Colin is actually bringing his own sand to the beach tonight! Doesn't he know that Anna's parties are crawling with beautiful single models!

After *Brokeback Mountain*, "brokeback" became the new term to describe "something that is gay," according to Urban Dictionary. And it's spread beyond English—according to the *Taipei Times*, "brokeback" has even entered Cantonese slang.

BROKEBACK

broccoli

Marijuana. Term used by rapper E-40.

Guy 1: I'm 'bout to blow my paycheck on some broccoli.

Guy 2: Can I smoke with you? I got five on it.

brocket

Using your bra as a pocket.

Man: Can you carry my cell?

Woman: I don't have any pockets.

Man: Put it in your bocket.

brohemian

Variation of the word brother combined with the term bohemian. Used to denote a close affiliate.

Person 1: Yo, how's it going, brohemian?

Person 2: Chillin', dawg, just lampin' it.

brokeback

1. Adjective used to describe anything of questionable masculinity. Derived from the film *Brokeback Mountain*.

Person 1: Dude, please tell me you are not wearing perfume!

Person 2: What? No . . . it's cologne . . . I swear!

Person 1: Well, it smells pretty brokeback to me.

bromance

The complicated love and affection shared by two straight males.

Steve: Ah, Dave! I can't believe you stole this first pressing of Aladdin Sane from your record store for me. We were just talking about this the other night. That is some full-on bromance. You're the man.

bromise

A promise that you really mean to keep.

I bromise I'll give you the money tomorrow, cuz I'm cool like that.

brownie

Term used to describe someone who has no qualifications for a high-level position. They are only in the position because they are a close friend, financial contributor, or ardent supporter of the person appointing them.

Brownie, you're doin' a heckuva job.

brown note

A low-octave sound that causes erratic bowel movements.

I heard the brown note and shit my pants.

brush the horse

When you are walking past someone in close proximity and your body parts touch theirs, making you feel uncomfortable.

Did that guy just brush the horse? I swear I felt his fupa on my back when he passed by me.

BTW

By the way.

I'm halfway to Minneapolis now. BTW, it's dangerous to text while driving.

bubble boy

Someone who's always sick.

Rick: Hey, Johnno, you coming out tonight?

John: Nah, I can't, I've got a sore throat.

Rick: You're such a bubble boy!

bubble wrap

The single most enjoyable plastic-based product on this earth. A sheet of thin plastic filled with air bubbles; endless hours of popping fun.

Med student: What should I prescribe for a patient for depression?

Doctor: Bubble wrap!

buck 50

A wound requiring at least 150 stitches.

Yo, you 'bout to catch a buck 50.

buckets

The rims on a vehicle.

I ride real slow, so they can see the buckets on mah feet.

buddha

Marijuana. Used to draw a parallel between the Buddha's state of nirvana and that cool, laidback feeling you get when you smoke a fat bowl.

Let's go smoke some buddha and get high as hell.

buddy pounce

IMing someone as soon as they sign on.

As soon as his name appeared on my buddy list I buddy pounced him.

buddy punch

When a person at work clocks in ("punches in") their friend when their friend is late to work.

Person 1: Did you clock in for Stevie?

Person 2: Oh, yes. Good old buddy punch!

Bueller

Used as filler when nobody responds to a question or statement. A reference to the movie *Ferris Bueller's Day Off.*

Person 1: Has anybody seen my hat?

Person 2: . . .

Person 1: Bueller?

buffet pants

A form of pantslike clothing in which the waistband is made of elastic for easy expansion of the abdomen.

Hey, Ross, let's put our buffet pants on and go to Mandarin Gourmet.

bulla

An English slang word short for "bullshit."

Person 1: Someone told me that Thierry Henry has signed for Scunthorpe United?!

Person 2: Nah, man, that's bulla.

bumper

A booty, typically a female's.

Pull up to my bumper.

bumper sticker

A small free-speech zone that can be placed on the back of a car. All varieties of crude and rude attitudes can be displayed on a bumper sticker. While some supposedly funny quotes are placed on some, most immediately lose their hilarity due to repeated use. Bumper stickers can also be used to attempt to change tailgaters' opinions.

I sure hope my "Jesus Loves You" bumper sticker converts that guy in the Volvo!

bumpin'

1. A term used for music when played at a high volume.

2. A complimentary adjective.

Yo, dude, that new stereo system of yours is bumpin'!

bun

London/U.K. term meaning to smoke marijuana/hashish; derived from the word "burn."

Do you bun? We have been bunning.

bunched

To be upset or angry; to have one's panties in a bunch.

Sally's bunched because she doesn't have a date to the dance.

bunny boiler

Clingy, possessive, overbearing, psycho bitch of a girlfriend (think *Fatal Attraction*).

Man, I can't believe Kate. Since we broke up, she keeps ringing my place and hanging up when I answer. She turned into a bunny boiler for real.

bunnyhug
A zipperless hooded sweatshirt with a pocket in front.

She pulled on her bunnyhug because she was cold.

BUO
Break-upable offense.

She farted in the middle of having sex. That was a total BUO.

burner
1. A handgun.

Darzel took the burner to school because there was a gang after him.

2. A throwaway prepaid cell phone, typically used by dealers. Used until the minutes are up, then thrown away so they cannot be tapped.

There are burners all over the street.

burn victim
Someone who smokes large amounts of marijuana and lacks intelligence because of it; aka "burnout."

You don't remember your girlfriend's birthday, Chase? You're such a burn victim!

burrow
To lounge or to be lazy in a cold,

dark environment, maybe while watching a movie.

I'm tired. I'm gonna go burrow.

bush pig
A wholly unattractive female.

Your mom really is a bit of a bush pig.

business/bizness
A bad beating or ass whooping.

If that kid keeps talkin' 'bout me I'm gonna give him tha business.

bus left
Missing the bus.

I got bus left this morning.

bus look
A blank facial expression (somewhat similar to a poker face) used while riding a bus. A person sustaining a bus look is often deep in thought or examining the surrounding people. Off the bus, this can be considered acting stoic.

I boarded on the J downtown and smiled at the trendy cute girl, but she was too absorbed in her bus look to notice me.

bust a free
A hip-hop term meaning rap free-styling; producing multiple rhyming phrases in sequence off the top of one's head with little or no preparation time.

Yo, Andre, show these niggas how to rap and bust a free on their asses.

bust a nut

To be overcome with an intense amount of emotion.

When I heard the news, I nearly busted a nut.

bustday

The day you realize your NCAA bracket is busted, and you're probably not going to win the pool unless somehow a double-digit team wins the title.

Looks like someone's got a case of the bustdays.

bust up

Beat the hell out of.

I'm going to bust up her pimp; he deserves to get beat up.

bus victim

1. Waking up with a hangover or feeling like hell and looking it, too.

I raged all night and when I got up this

morning, I felt like a bus victim!

2. Subjected to riding a bus.

I was a bus victim today when my Land Rover wouldn't start.

butter bar

Military slang for ensign or second lieutenant, who wears a golden bar as their rank insignia.

Who's the new butter bar in charge?

butterface

Fine body . . . but her face gotta go! Also "butterhead."

Did ya peep out da butterhead on aisle five?

butterfaith

A girl who is fun, intelligent, beautiful and perfect in every way . . . except she's devoutly religious.

If not for the whole going-to-church-and-not-eating-meat-on-Fridays thing, Jenny would be perfect. Too bad she's a butterfaith.

butterlung

Excessive cotton mouth due to the inhalation of the sweet, sweet ganja.

Dude, that last rip gave me hella butterlung.

butt hurt

Getting your feelings hurt or getting all bent out of shape.

He got all butt hurt when she wouldn't give him a ride.

butt monkey

Someone who worships another person. They laugh at all their jokes whether they're funny or not, they think they're great even when they're not, and generally strive to spend as much time with that person as they can. The person the butt-monkeys follow is called a butt-monkey king or queen.

Jones is such a kiss-ass butt monkey.

buttmunch

Someone who is a source of irritation, thus becoming the target of another's animosity. Synonyms: jerk, wanker, bastard, creep, asshole, shithead.

All you do is make fun of me. You're such a buttmunch.

butt puppet

A person or figurehead who speaks under the direction of another, as though a child's sock toy with someone's arm jammed up their ass.

Why bother listening to Jack? He's like totally Natalie's butt puppet.

buzz back

To respond or reply to, especially regarding email, IM, etc.

Hey, we should go do something tonight. Buzz back if you have any ideas.

buzzin'

Really happy.

I'm proper buzzin'.

BWAM

Acronym for "boner with a motive." Term used when a male has an erection after seeing someone sexually attractive.

She was gorgeous, so right away there was a BWAM.

bya

The word "bye" and "cya" slurred together; similar to "heylo."

Lillian: I've gotta go, Ross. :)

Ross: Alright, bya!

bye loop

What happens when, on the phone or instant messenger, someone needs to leave (or fakes needing to go to end the conversation) and says "bye" (or an IM variant like "cya").

The other participant says "bye" or something, then the original person says "bye/whatever" again, and the other one responds. This can go on for minutes or longer until someone—or their parent—puts their foot down.

babyC8KS: well I g2g

babyC8KS: cya

SK8rboi: cya

babyC8KS: bye

SK8rboi: call you later

babyC8KS: l8r

SK8rboi: yea, cya

babyC8KS: ttyt

SK8rboi: g2g

babyC8KS: cya

SK8rboi: bye~~~

babyC8KS: OK I HAVE TO GO NOW!!! PARENTS!!! GAH! BYE!

SK8rboi: OK!!! BYE!!!

by proxy
The ability to do or be something without actually physically doing it.

Sarah lives with a smoker, so when they watch TV together she smokes by proxy.

dictionary

C

c2c

Cam-to-cam. Online interaction where both parties are visible to each other via a webcam. Sometimes used for simple conversations, but most often for exhibitionistic/ voyeuristic remote sex. Usually seen in terms of a proposition in a chat room.

My webcam is on, any horny ladies want to join me for c2c?

cabana boy

A young man (typically in his twenties) who gives a woman anything and everything she needs or wants, as a servant would. Most of her needs or wants have a sexual connotation.

I was at the beach and the cabana boy massaged my feet as I drank my piña colada.

cabbage

Cash money. Mo' money.

Yo, you got any cabbage?

cable spaghetti

The series of cords needed to run your life by connecting all your computer equipment, entertainment devices, and lamps. Cable spaghetti can be recognized by its nexus at a surge protector. Wireless devices are represented in the spaghetti by their various rechargers, none of which are compatible.

I had to deal with the cable spaghetti behind my desk to add speakers to my computer at work.

cached

The state of completion a pipe or other smoking device reaches once all the substance within it is reduced to ash.

Stoner 1: Dude, pass the dutchie.

Stoner 2: Can't, man, it's cached.

cack

One of the many alternative words the British have for shit.

That film was total cack.

cacked

1. Totally screwed up, broken, shit.

Goddamnit, this computer is completely cacked.

2. Covered and completely screwed because of it.

Ha ha! You fell over and landed in pig shit. You're cacked with shit!

cack your pants

To crap your pants.

I thought you were going to cack your pants when your girlfriend told you she was pregnant.

caddywhip

The act of taking a wide, slow turn in a car, first partially steering to the wrong direction (left, if turning right) then changing the steering back to the desired direction; aka "G turn." A term coined because a big Cadillac takes up a lot of road when turning.

Hey, bust a caddywhip and go down Main Street.

Cadillac mack

A person who rolls in their clean, plush Cadillac, with hoes walking up to the car door to holla. Haters, and people with Lincolns, usually detest this person.

The Cadillac mack is always pimpin', never simpin', that's how it is.

Cadillac Republican

Most leaders of the Republican Party. Rich; smoke cigars in smoke-filled rooms; evil liars. They take advantage of the Chevrolet Republicans.

Karl Rove is a Cadillac Republican.

cafediem

Caffeinate the day.

To ask someone if they want a coffee, one would say, "Cafediem?"

caffeine toxic

Extremely intoxicated with caffeine.

Chris: Holy shit, B, you're really caffeine toxic. I'll go get the spatula.

Stef: *Stuck to ceiling*

caffeine whore

A person who cannot function without regular caffeine fixes; a person who drinks most of the coffee in the coffee room, leaving none for anybody else; a person who will borrow money or steal coffee just to get a fix of the sweet bitter black.

There's no coffee left. That caffeine whore drank it all.

cager

A term used by motorcyclists to describe someone driving a four-wheeled vehicle.

That cager just cut me off!

cain't

Synonym for the contraction "can't."

Man, a nigga cain't getta break.

cajungly

Crazy, out of order; in a chaotic state.

Ever since he has been on drugs, his life has been cajungly.

cake

1. A kilo of cocaine.

Did you cut that cake?

2. To flirt or cupcake.

Aw, I saw your girlfriend in the hallway! Her and Ronald was cakin' they asses off!

cake daddy

A male totally consumed with his female partner. A cake daddy will abandon his friends and spend all of his time with said female.

Man, he turned cake daddy on us and spends all his time with his girl.

cake-eaters

Rich people, especially those who go out of their way to show off their wealth.

I drove by the country club yesterday, and all the cake-eaters were lined up to play eighteen.

California divorce

When a married couple from California get divorced, but still have sex with each other.

The terms of Jim and Jane's California divorce include Jim paying alimony and child support and sleeping with Jane on the weekends.

California king

An overly arrogant, highly egotistical self-made man; full of himself and unaware of anything that does not directly relate to him. Has a use-and-throw-away-policy regarding women. Primarily from the Golden State, but they have been known to migrate.

What an asshole. He's such a California king!

California turn signal

Flipping the bird, usually to another driver, either upon witnessing an act of pure idiocy or during road rage.

That old fart is doing 20 under the limit in the carpool lane. Give 'im the California turn signal, will ya?

camel hump

When the balls are visible through tight pants.

Those pants were tight like no other; they gave Elvis a camel hump.

camel toe

When her pants are so tight you can read her lips!

Oh, man, her pants were so tight I could see her camel toe.

cam whore

A female on the Internet who exposes herself on her webcam to large numbers of horny bastards.

I broke up with Sherry because that slut is a cam whore.

Canadian boyfriend/ girlfriend

An imaginary or fictional boyfriend or girlfriend.

Vince: Trevor, why haven't we met your girlfriend? You've been dating for over a year.

Trevor: She's really busy.

Vince: Oh, yeah, I forgot how busy Canadians can be.

Trevor: What?

Mike: Vince is just saying you've got a Canadian girlfriend, that's all.

canary

To run a yellow light.

Man, I'm just missing the green wave. I keep canary-ing these lights.

cancer chancer

One who smokes and therefore risks contracting cancer.

I used to be a cancer chancer, twenty times a day.

C and E

People who show up at church only on Christmas and Easter.

Better set up more chairs in the sanctuary so all the C and E folks have a place to sit.

candy flip

The combination of LSD and Ecstasy; to take such a combination.

What's that in my coffee? A candy flip!

candy paint

A high-gloss paint finish applied to automobiles.

Dat candy paint be shining like Christmas on da 'lac.

can you not

Fragment often used by girls to thwart further activity; please stop; that ain't right; don't do that, because I don't like it.

Jon pokes Jane. Jane says, "Can you not?"

cap

To front; to say stuff that isn't true.

She said she won $1,000 yesterday. Why is she cappin'? She knows she ain't got no money.

carbucks

The coffee stains around the front-seat carpet in most cars. Impossible to completely clean.

I forgot that my venti was in the cup holder, took a sharp turn, and got carbucks all over.

cardiocracy

Democracy in physical action; when you "vote with your feet"; whenever free-expression about politics involves walking or running.

This caucus is pure cardiocracy!

care police

A police organization formed for people who do not want to hear others whine about meaningless and random occurrences that happen in their boring lives.

You owe your dealer how much, sweetie? Someone call the care police.

carriage-cruiser

A person who is unable to simply stand in one position on a train and decides, much to the annoyance of the other passengers, to move down the length of the train using the internal doors.

I was standing in the corridor of the 8:24 train and I had no fewer than six carriage-cruisers squeeze past me.

carrot

A promised improvement or change that never happens, usually in the workplace. A form of bait used to keep the interest of a naive/trusting person.

They say things will get better when we get the new front office system, but it's just another carrot!

carry it

To tell someone to get out of your face and leave. The idea is that you're telling them to take, i.e., carry, their personal baggage and get out of your presence.

You best carry it on out of here.

carsophagus

1. A pothole in the road that is so large that it could eat a car. This is a play on the word "sarcophagus," which literally means "body eater."

He drove into a carsophagus created by the spring freezing and thawing, and the car's front wheel alignment was ruined.

2. A hearse or other vehicle used for carrying the dead.

I had a friend that would drive the carsophagus at funerals.

carspective

The valuable insight that comes during the long drive home.

Dude, I totally figured out our budget problem. I got some carspective driving home last night.

case

To slip, fall, or generally injure yourself while either drunk or sober.

Dude, I cased on that ice.

case of the Mondays

A weekly sickness that affects students and workers. Symptoms include a useless or horrible Monday morning and being really pissed off.

10:15 a.m.: At work suffering from a case of the Mondays.

cash and prizes

Your junk, privates, twig and berries, ouch.

She kneed me right in the cash and prizes and took me to the ground.

cashectomy

Unplanned expenditure of money on some suddenly essential service.

A tree falling on your house on Christmas night may cause a $700 cashectomy.

casino air

The air you breathe inside a casino. Casino air is highly oxygenated and causes you to have high energy. The effects of alcohol and other

substances is enhanced. You'll never get tired living on casino air.

E: Yo, Dio, I'll be down at 11 p.m. Friday.

Dio: Aight . . . bring some Cîroc and Red Bull.

E: No need for the Red Bull. Once I get a hit of the casino air, I'll be good to go.

casket sharp

Extremely well dressed, as when people are buried in their sharpest suit.

Guy 1: You ready to pick up the girls for prom?

Guy 2: Yeah—I'm casket sharp.

Casper

A pale white kid who cannot get a tan. If in the sun too long, skin will turn red. Also: "ghost." Sometimes made fun of by acting like he is invisible.

Girl 1: Oh my God! Look at Casper! He's so damn white!

Girl 2: Where is he? I can't see him.

castle ass

The severe gastrointestinal disturbance that follows the consumption of a large volume of White Castle burgers, especially a ten-sack of cheeseburgers.

Castle ass is the number-one killer of

young adult males in Wisconsin.

casual undertime

Getting paid for forty hours for the week when one has worked less than forty hours. It is best when casual undertime is achieved by legitimate means, such as leaving early for the 4th of July holiday with your boss's permission.

I work casual undertime during the work-week before a three-day weekend: I usually can leave four hours early on Friday and still be paid for them.

catastrafuck

What happens when a cataclysm hits a hellhole. As used by Jon Stewart on *The Daily Show* October 3, 2006.

Did you hear about that earthquake in Sudan? What a catastrafuck!

catch and release

The practice of hooking up with someone and not becoming emotionally/physically attached to them.

Ben: Yo, I nailed this girl last night.

Dave: So are you going to call her later?

Ben: Hell no, man. I practice catch and release. That way, you can have a shot with her next weekend.

Dave: Thanks, Ben. You are a great person and a noble gentleman.

catch a square

To engage in a fight. Originated from the fact that boxing rings, where fights occur, are square.

It is just a matter of minutes before the fish in the cellblock has to prove he's 'bout it and catch a square.

cave rave

A party where the majority of attendees are female; the opposite of a "sausage fest."

Person 1: Who's gonna be at the party tonight?

Person 2: Tammy, Sarah, Laura, Monifa, Shaniqua . . . sounds like a real cave rave.

celebracy

The curious practice where a celebrity takes a vow of voluntary celibacy. Usually taken by brooding male rock stars like Rivers Cuomo and Morrissey.

I don't know why you'd practice celebracy when you could get any screaming teenage groupie you wanted.

celebreviate

The act of combining two celebrities' names because they are dating, married, etc.

People celebreviate for every couple in Hollywood these days: Bennifer—Ben Affleck and Jennifer Lopez; TomKat—Tom Cruise and Katie Holmes; Brangelina—Brad Pitt and Angelina Jolie.

celebutard

A famous stupid person; typically refers to the current crop of vapid celebrities.

Celebutard Paris Hilton got the name of her own videogame wrong.

Time magazine cited "celebutard" as one of the neologisms that "got people talking in 2006." They mentioned Paris Hilton, but they didn't know that she would really earn the title in 2007. See also "celebutante" and "professional celebrity" on urbandictionary.com.

CELEBUTARD

cellhole

A person using a cell phone while being completely oblivious to their surroundings, other people, or tasks requiring full and immediate attention.

The ring tone in the theater indicated there was a cellhole in the audience.

cell it

When people want you to call their cell.

Cell it later, bro. I gotta talk to you about the girl.

cell phone

A device for communicating with others needlessly. Day in. Day out.

Whenever. Wherever. Good for holding up lines in stores, traffic, etc.

Typical cell phone conversation:

Person 1: Hey, where you at?

Person 2: I'm over here.

Person 1: Oh.

Person 2: What?

Person 1: I dunno. I'll be there in 5 seconds. . . . Oh wait, I can see you! Hey! What's up? Wait . . . let me call you back.

Person 2: Why?

Person 1: Huh? Can you hear me? Guess what? My phone bill was only $90 this month.

cellular faux

Shielding yourself from an uncomfortable social situation by pretending to be on your cell phone.

When Peggy saw the bum approaching, she flipped open her LG and began laughing as though someone had told a joke on the other end of the line. Still penniless, the bum's plan was thwarted by cellular faux.

cell yell

The result of a person feeling that they need to drastically raise their voice in order to be heard on their mobile phone. Offenders of cell yell are oblivious to the fact that this is not necessary, and are often an extreme nuisance to everyone around them.

We had a hard time enjoying our meal at the restaurant, due to the cell yell of the woman at the next table.

chacha

Girl; derived from the Spanish word *muchacha,* meaning "girl."

Hey, chacha, you look damn good!

chair ass

The slow growth and spread of a clerical worker's physical frame after years of combining vending machine snack food with an exercise regimen that consists of little more than typing, until said physical frame is confined by the spatial limitations of the worker's desk chair. Commonly applies to programmers, secretaries, and middle management. In extreme cases, can be accompanied by a not-insignificant amount of physical exertion to free the compressed rear end from the chair.

She was really slender and athletic, before she started doing data entry sixty hours a week. But after all those late nights and candy bars, she's got a real case of chair ass.

chalupa

Money. Preferably a lot.

My occupation? I'm a hustla, gettin' chalupa.

champagne supernova

A martini glass full of champagne with cocaine on the rim, as salt would be on a margarita.

Make me a champagne supernova, please.

chanceability

A combination of chance and possibility. Means something that is likely to happen.

There is a high chanceability of me watching porn tomorrow.

charge it to the game

Similar to a "party foul." Something caused by fate that can't be altered.

I failed that test today. Oh well, charge it to the game.

chat gravity

The degree of familiarity with another person, which, if you chance to encounter them on the street, will determine if you merely greet them in passing or stop to talk.

We saw each other on the sidewalk and said "hello." But she was just a friend of a friend I'd only met once or twice before, and there wasn't enough chat gravity to merit a stop and chat.

chat junkie

One who spends all day on AIM, MSN, Yahoo!, or Google chat. They don't have social lives outside it and generally don't care.

Trillian, OMG, she's such a chat junkie. I wonder how long she could go without an Internet connection.

chatspeak

A form of speech in which one shortens words and replaces the letter "s" with the letter "z." Chatspeak rarely uses capitalization or punctuation.

Examples:
boys—boiz
girls—girlz, grlz, grrlz, gurlz
mate—m8
skater—sk8er
you—u
are—r
tonight—2nite
because—bcuz

hi im a grrl how r u??? ok so dont talk 2 me i dont care!!!

chav

In England, a delinquent. A person who does not believe in banks and thus retains funds as gold-plated jewelry.

Look at the twenty inchers on me Nova, it's well phat, innit! Bling bling!

check

To put someone in their place.

Best check yo' self, before you wreck yo' self.

checked baggage

Airliner lingo for someone with children.

Girl, don't mess with him, he's got checked baggage!

check my spam

Checking one's email though certain one has received no important communication. Compulsively and frequently checking one's email when one is not expecting an important message.

Between friends in a cybercafé:

Person 1: Hey, could you hurry up so I can get on and check my email?

Person 2: Who are you kidding, little bro, you know all your email buddies have dropped you like a brick!

Person 1: Yeah, I gotta check my spam . . . vamoose!

check your neck

A phrase used as a warning to be on the lookout for someone or a group of people who are going to attack you. Used mainly among prisoners and street hoods to instill fear in a rival gang member or person they dislike.

Best check your neck, son.

check your vitals

To check your email, MySpace, Facebook, blog, and/or any daily essential web sites.

Get off the computer. I need to check my vitals.

cheeky monkey

Originally used to define someone who gives a lot of lip and is a smart-ass, but now refers to anyone talking or behaving audaciously.

One of the girls spanked my perfectly curved butt, the cheeky monkey.

cheese & rice
Christian substitute for saying "Jesus Christ" in vain.

Bobby wipes out on his stingray bicycle:

Bobby: Owww! Cheese & rice! Dog bandit! Stupid frickin' bike!

chemical romance
Relationship or encounters based mainly on a controlled substance. Popularized by emo-music-type artists.

I'm glad I got out of that chemical romance.

chemical yoga
A chemical cocktail of Xanax and muscle relaxers, used in conjunction to relax one's mind and body.

I couldn't sleep last night, so I did some chemical yoga and it put my ass down.

cherry
1. The hymen.

Dude, she still has her cherry.

2. A virgin.

That girl's still cherry, dude.

3. Cool, good.

Dude, your new place is cherry, dude.

4. The burning ember of a cigarette, joint, or pipe.

That cherry fell off into your lap, dude.

5. Adjective to describe pot that doesn't need to be lit; also "cherried."

Don't spark that bowl, dude, it's cherry.

chesticles
Female breasts. Derived from the male word "testicles."

While playing softball, the woman playing third took a line drive right in the chesticles.

chevrolegs
Your feet. The kind of vehicle you own when you can't afford a car.

Girl: What kind of car you got?

Guy: I roll on '81 Chevrolegs.

Girl: Loser!

chewable
Someone who is way sexy and hot.

Nicole is so chewable in them short-shorts.

chibble
1. Marijuana.

Call Bob, maybe he knows where we can find some chibble.

2. To smoke marijuana.

Let's go over to Bone's house. Bring your pipe so we can chibble on the way.

chickchismo

1. A strong sense of womanly pride; an exaggerated femininity.

2. Exaggerated or exhilarating sense of female cunning and womanly wiles.

Blanche sure used her chickchismo to get what she wanted today!

chicken hawk

1. A gay term for an older man who constantly chases after younger men, typically in their twenties. The heterosexual female equivalent is the cougar.

Alberto is such a chicken hawk. He was hanging out at the coffee shop again trying to pick up skateboarders half his age!

2. A politician or other person who promotes war without having had any personal experience of it, especially those who have avoided the experience.

That draft-dodging chicken hawk has no business sending our children to war.

chick lit

Slang for a genre of literature geared toward female readers that deals with modern issues in women's lives.

The novel Bridget Jones's Diary *is an example of chick lit.*

chief

To spark a phatty bowl. To smoke marijuana with one's associates.

We should get together and chief later. I just scored a phatty sack of kind bud.

chimping

What one does after taking a picture with a digital camera and looking at the result. Derived from the words they speak: "Ooo-oo-oo!"

Tourists: Ooo-oo-oo! Look at Jane in front of the car! She's so pretty!

Locals: Stupid tourists and their stupid chimping.

chimple

Chin dimple.

Dude! Ben Affleck's got a huge chimple.

chimplify

Simplification to the extreme; making something so simple a monkey could understand it. Usually made in reference to a clueless employer.

Person 1: I just got finished presenting my ideas to Jim.

Person 2: How did it go?

Person 1: OK, I just had to chimplify it.

chinglish

Speaking both English and Chinese in one's sentences.

Example of a sentence in chinglish: "At K-mart, I buy hen duo clothes."

chippie

Cheap, common, sexually promiscuous girl, wearing way too much makeup and shiny cheap jewelry, usually underage or close to it.

Don't wear that outfit. That miniskirt with the hot-pink lipstick and inch of black eyeliner on your eyes makes you look like a chippie.

chirps
To chat up.

Dem manz spend all their time tryin' to chirps females.

chizzle
The act of hanging out; aka "chillin'," "chilling."

Phone rings.

Person 1: Hello?

Person 2: I'm bored, wanna chizzle?

chizzler
One who continually "mooches" or uses others to acquire goods or services.

Buy your own beer, you chizzler!

choon
Song, tune; originally from reggae/dancehall culture, it has also been adopted by the drum and bass scene (which has been heavily influenced by Jamaican music).

'Tis a right wicked choon dat de selecta be playin'.

chop
To have sex with.

I would definitely chop her.

choppers
Candy-coated rims twenty-six inches in diameter; dubs = 20s, twanks = 22s, jordans = 23s, grown men = 24s, choppers = 26s.

Got choppers?

Chrismukkah
The holiday mixture of Hanukkah and Christmas for those who come from a mixed Christian and Jewish background. Its origin is the Fox television show *The O.C.*

Happy Chrismukkah: Eight days of presents, followed by one day of many presents.

Christmas creep
A phenomenon where the Christmas season starts earlier and earlier each year.

If they don't keep the Christmas creep under control, the season will start in June.

Christmas cringe
The feeling of sudden and impending doom after receiving a gift from a coworker or classmate in spite of the fact that you have nothing in common except that you are coworkers or classmates. This gift is always generic, pointless, useless,

and frequently related to some sort of poshlust fad.

Anna from the front row actually stood there and made me open it in front of her. I couldn't hide my Christmas cringe, so now she's telling everyone what a bitch I am for not liking the light-up reindeer socks she gave me.

Christmas gear

The new clothes that people received for the holidays. Usually worn the first week in January and recognized by the new clothes smell and creases left from being folded in boxes since Thanksgiving.

Steve wore his Christmas gear on his first day back from winter break and all the cool kids teased him about his shoes.

Christmess

The aftermath of Christmas celebrations.

We had a great day, but it was a nightmare cleaning up all that Christmess afterward.

chronchitis

Bronchitis you get after smoking marijuana nonstop for a long-ass time, like when you're stoned all week. Symptoms include excessive nasty-sounding coughs and haziness. Cure: lay off the bud.

Goddamn, dude, we shouldn't have smoked that whole lid at once. I think I got chronchitis.

chronic

1. Very high-quality weed, generally with red hairs on it.

2. A long-lasting medical condition.

From smoking too much chronic, Joe ended up with a chronic case of the shaky-shivers.

chronoptimist

A person who always underestimates the time necessary to do something or get somewhere.

Neil: Hey, Cindy, you know my parents are expecting us in twenty minutes.

Cindy: No problem. I just have to wash the dishes, take a shower, do my hair, and walk the dog, and then I'm all good to go. See you in fifteen.

Neil: You are such a chronoptimist! I'll see you in forty-five.

chronovore

Derived from Greek "chronos" (time) + Latin "vore" (eating). Any of a variety of time-consuming and potentially addictive toys, games, or activities. Especially apt for computer games and web surfing.

I was going to go to bed at ten, but World of Warcraft is such a chronovore, I was up until 3 a.m.

chubby chaser

A person who is attracted to overweight people; one who likes chunky monkeys.

Tom is a chubby chaser; he only really wants heavy women.

chuch

A word usually used at the end of a sentence to express agreement and/or excitement; similar to the word "Amen."

We gotta roll down to that bitch crib. But first let's finish this fat-ass blunt. Chuch!

chumped

To be ripped off or to be made to look like a chump.

Man, I got chumped by that scam artist.

chunk the deuce

1. To display the peace sign as in saying "later." Also: "throw the deuce," "deuces."

He chunked up the deuce to his boys as he left the house.

2. Term used to say "I'm outtie."

I had to chunk the deuce early to that gay-ass party last night.

churched

Kinda like "you got served," except it's much better. No one really likes the church; when you get churched, you got dissed and nobody likes you.

Damn, man! That sucka emcee just got churched!

chyea

A positive response to a question, like "Yea" but with more enthusiasm; a chant to get pumped up before getting crunk.

Person 1: Do u want to get crunk?

Person 2: Chyea!

CI

Confidential informant; any individual under the direction of a police officer who furnishes information about criminal activity with or without compensation; works under direction of the department; different from other concerned citizens or complainants not working under department direction and not party to the investigation itself.

My CI places you and your homies at the Qwik-E-Mart last night when the shootings occurred.

cigaweed

When you empty out all the tobacco from a cigarette and fill it up with weed because you can't roll a good blunt, or when you stuff weed into a cigarette with some tobacco still inside.

Person 1: Why do you have all those cigs?

Person 2: Because every time I roll a blunt all my shit falls out, so I have to make cigaweed.

Cinderella

In sports, specifically the playoffs, a Cinderella is a team that does better than expected near the beginning and then quickly fades.

A true Cinderella story: A thirteen seed gets into the sweet sixteen of the NCAA Basketball Tournament and is destroyed by an eight seed.

cinderfella

A guy who cleans all the time; a man-bitch you make clean up all the time either just because, or for payment of booze, food, and other things he mooches off you.

Mike is my cinderfella because he's broke and I'm lazy!

cinematard

One who is completely lacking movie knowledge.

Hey, Greta, wanna see that new Tom Hanks movie, Mission: Difficult II?

cinemuck

The combination of popcorn, soda, and melted chocolate that covers the floors of movie theaters.

Dude, are you sure you wanna wear those kicks to the theater? You know what cinemuck will do to your shoes.

cinesleaze

General term given to any low-budget film designed to attract audiences with an abundant amount of nudity. Particularly used to describe soft-core pornography on late-night premium cable channels.

The cinesleaze we watched last night had plenty of beautiful girls running around with nothing on!

circle pit

Can be noun or verb. A form of violent, aggressive dancing or "slamming" during punk shows that stays within the confines of an open circular area in the middle of the floor. Any of the following may occur within the circle pit:

1. Dancing or skanking that looks like running in a counterclockwise fashion;

2. Random thrashing with elbows swinging and legs kicking out in a "running man" style;

3. The pogo, or hopping up and down and bumping into other

participants, usually at the front of the floor.

Dude, I'm so sore from all those punks slam-dancing in the circle pit last night at the Circle Jerks show!

circle talker

A person who continually forgets what was just asked and asks the same question repeatedly. Usually associated with a medicated person.

Bob: How long were you there?

Gil: About ten minutes.

Bob: Really?

Gil: Yes.

Bob: So how long were you probably there?

circumfornicate

To waste time. A cute way of saying "fuck around." Akin to "circumflatulate," but harsher and harder to explain in polite company.

Would you idiots quit circumfornicating and get back to work?

Clark Kent job

Your day job, or a job that pays the bills but is not what you really want to do.

What's your Clark Kent job?

clear it

To leave an area, to vacate.

Person 1: Y'all still at the party?

Person 2: Yeah, but it's kind of dead. We're about to clear it.

cleat chaser

A promiscuous woman who follows athletes (baseball or football) usually on the college level, in the hopes of having intercourse with one of them.

Yo, that bitch is a cleat chaser. The whole team has nailed her.

clicktease

When a web site leads you to believe you will be seeing pornography or some other sexual material, when in fact this offer is false or misleading.

Man, I thought that email was totally my ticket to free porn, but it ended up just being home loans and pay sites! What a clicktease!

clip show

A sorry excuse to extend the season of a show by using preexisting clips from the show in a nostalgic manner.

American Idol's a clip show tonight, so you can safely skip it.

clitteratti

A group of lesbians, famous or in the limelight, who are photographed extensively.

The clitteratti were out in full force at the film festival.

CLM

Career-limiting move.

Kissing his boss's wife turned out to be a CLM for Hank.

clocksucker

Someone who wastes tremendous amounts of your time with no useful result.

After two years of dating, he didn't propose, the clocksucker!

clog

A pedestrian who monopolizes shared walkways with complete inconsideration of others. Most often used to describe a lackadaisical walker who blocks other, more agile, pedestrians from getting to where they need to go or one of a larger group of lunchtime strollers who think it's cute to walk shoulder-to-shoulder, five or six in a row, on a busy city sidewalk.

Don't these clogs know what it means to walk single file?

closed for repairs

The time during which a girl/guy is getting over some kind of sexual illness/injury and can't or won't have sex.

Julie's yeast infection was horrific. She was closed for repairs for so long!

CLM

Michael Richards's CLM made waves on Urban Dictionary in 2006, when he responded angrily to hecklers during a live performance in Los Angeles. The following week, Urban Dictionary published a definition for "kramered": "to be called out and berated, often based on your ethnicity, in a public setting."

closet freak

A lady in the streets and a freak in the sheets.

Freddie hooked up with Jenny, the closet freak.

clown car it

When more people than there are seatbelts are shoved into a car. People have to sit on the floor or on each other.

Kelly was driving; Becky had shotgun; Ashley, Kelsey, Jay, and Mandee were in back with Ashley sitting on Mandee and Jay sitting on Kelsey. I had to sit on Becky. We were so clown car-ing it.

clown poop

Styrofoam packing "peanuts," specifically the white variety.

As I opened my box from the Home Shopping Network, a strong gust of wind blew the clown poop all over the yard.

club couple

A couple that begins their relationship with drunken sex after meeting in a club, then awkwardly attempts to make a go of things in the nonclub world. These couples typically find that they only feel comfortable going on more club dates and simply can't function in other scenarios. Estimated time to expiration: one to two weeks. Very, very uncomfortable weeks.

At a restaurant:

Club couple dude: So . . . uh . . . Jennifer, do you play sports and stuff?

Club couple broad: My name is Jeannette.

(Cue the most awkward silence possible.)

clucky

When a woman is feeling broody, which means she is starting to see babies, and all that having one entails, in a much more positive light. She may start mentioning things like her "biological clock" and maybe even do something as drastic as stop taking the pill in order to satisfy her maternal urges.

Boyfriend discovers girlfriend's pill packet:

Oh dear God . . . She's skipped the last WEEK! Please don't tell me she's feeling clucky!

cluster fuck

Military term for a situation caused by too many inept officers, "cluster"

referring to the oak leaf clusters insignia worn by majors and lieutenant colonels.

The planning for this operation was a complete cluster fuck.

coaster

A disc received from America Online. Since using the program is a waste of time, it is better to use them as coasters to set your drinks on, lest you damage a wood or other valuable surface.

I got so many AOL 9.0 coasters last month I glued them to my ceiling and now it's shiny, disco-style.

cock block

One who prevents another from scoring sexually.

Trudy and Dan frequently had time together but her cock-blocking roommate ruined any chances they had to have sex.

cocktail flu

The "illness" that you have after a full night of drinking; what you tell your boss you have, when calling in sick the next day.

I had to call in with the cocktail flu after we went out all night and ran the bar out of Jägermeister. Oh, my aching hair!

code monkey

An affectionate term for a specific kind of underpaid, overworked (often by their own volition), increasingly underappreciated indentured servant otherwise known as a software programmer. Derived from the Latin-Greek "codex" and the obsolete-Japanese "Donkey Kong-San."

Socrates says we're all just expendable code monkeys, sitting here in the late Tokugawa period.

code of the road

1. The rule that every driver on earth believes that anyone driving slower than they are is an idiot and those driving faster must be assholes.

Look at this idiot driving fifty. Holy shit! Did you see that asshole?!

2. An unspoken rule that what-ever happens on a road trip is not repeated to anyone except those involved in the road trip.

Marc could not tell Paul's wife what happened on the way to New York because of the code of the road.

coffee snob

Going well beyond the utility of using coffee as a morning stimulant, the coffee snob has made their favorite mug or grande Starbucks cup a fashion accessory. Coffee snobs are usually seen with their coffee at about chest-level, so everyone can see the chosen beverage accessory, and are unusually reluctant to put it down for any reason.

Driver: Why are we stuck at this green light?

Passenger: The coffee snob in that SUV is trying to parallel park that sled with one hand.

coin

Money; dollar bills.

You've got a good gig! I bet you make some decent coin.

coke nail

A superlong pinkie nail. Derived from the term used by druggies to sniff coke.

Hey, I just broke my coke nail. I was really liking it, too.

coke whites

Another term for Air Force Ones made by Nike; mentioned in the song "Vans" by the Pack.

I've got ten pairs of these joints, my icy coke whites.

cold cock

The act of punching or striking someone's face or head so hard, they are knocked out instantly.

Dude! Greg was in this wicked bar fight, and he got totally cold cocked by a biker!

Colgate kiss

A kiss after one of the participants has just brushed their teeth.

He kissed me last night right after he brushed his teeth. It tasted horrible.

collabo

Collaboration.

Dat Ciara and Ludacris collabo was off da chain!

colonary

Food that, when consumed, results in a complete colon cleansing.

Taco Bell is a colonary hot spot.

comatoast

So toasted you're practically in a coma.

Man, I'm comatoast since we roasted that bowl.

combat buzz

Drinking to a point where you are not impaired but have lost some feeling in the body to gain an edge in a fight; drinking to not feel physical pain.

Even though Mike hit Dan repeatedly in the stomach and face, Dan did not feel it because of his combat buzz.

come to Jesus

Originally an emotional experience that is life changing, it has evolved to mean a serious argument, one that better result in a change of action or else.

I'm going to have a come to Jesus with that kid about his drinking and partying.

coming in hot

Having to use the restroom in a dire manner as you arrive at your destination; to head straight for the bathroom after getting out of the car.

After eating at that Mexican restaurant, Ray was coming in hot.

command Z

To undo an action that's taken place in the real world. Command Z originated life as keyboard shortcut for "undo."

Oops, I've reversed over that lady on the Zimmer frame in my large SUV. I'd better command Z it.

commentversation

Having a conversation through blog comments.

Comment from Garrett: What are you doing right now?

Comment from Jay: Nothing.

Comment from Kelly: Your mom.

Comment from Garrett: Oooo, good one.

Comment from Jay: That's so mean!

Comment from Garrett: You're mean.

Comment from Jay: No I'm not!

Comment from Garrett: Just kidding! I love you.

Comment from Jay: I love you, too!

comment whore

On blogs, a person who posts something for the sole purpose of gaining comments (usually positive) from other users.

Carolyn, a well-known comment whore, always posts surveys for her friends to fill out.

commercide

When an e-commerce site is so slow that you just can't buy anything from them.

The store site was so slow the other night they committed commercide, so I just left and bought someplace else.

condescenti

Pseudo-intellectuals who try to make you feel uncool.

The J. T. Leroy book signing in SoHo last night was crawling with condescenti. I nearly barfed.

condomplating

The act of deliberating whether it is worth it to run to the store in the middle of the night to buy a condom. Alcohol is usually involved.

She asked me if I wanted to sleep with her or on the couch, and I said I'm condomplating.

connectile dysfunction

The inability to gain or maintain an Internet connection, or the inability to print, email, or get to the Internet.

My computer had connectile dysfunction yesterday, so I couldn't check my email.

conversational puma

A loud and opportunistic member of a conversation. The "puma" part comes from the person's tendency to "pounce" on you when you are trying to tell a story with loud interjections like "No way" or "I *know*." Though it's debatable whether the conversational puma is truly interested in what you are saying or if he/she is just patronizing you, the story usually ends up being truncated for no other reason than to avoid being loudly interrupted. Used on the radio program *Loveline* by Adam Carolla.

Jesus Christ, I hate that Suzy. I can't finish a single sentence without her pouncing on me with "OMG" or something like that. She's such a conversational puma.

conversation jailer

One who won't stop talking, typically in a social scene. The type of person you make up an excuse to get away from.

Sorry I wasn't back earlier, but that conversation jailer Eddie wouldn't shut up.

cook by numbers

A meal that requires nothing more than pushing numbers on the microwave; oftentimes a frozen dinner or leftovers.

Mark's parents were out of town, so he had to cook by numbers.

corporate fluffer
A person who excels in a company simply by sucking up or being a kiss-ass.

Oh, him? He got to the top by being a corporate fluffer. Another one of those, "the employees have to be qualified, but the managers don't."

cosigner
Someone who goes along with or corroborates someone else's lie in order to cover for them.

Without even giving me a heads-up, he told his mom that he had been at my house all night. I cosigned for him because we're close.

couch commando
An individual (usually a male) who takes the television remote control and won't let anyone change the channel or take it from them.

Quit being a couch commando. I want to watch Cops.

couching distance
The distance one can reach without leaving the couch or sofa.

That job is too far; it's not within couching distance.

couchlock
Too stoned to get off of the couch.

That ganj had us in couchlock for four hours.

courage dot com
When someone tries to be badass over the Internet, like on a forum or blog, because they aren't actually face-to-face with anyone.

DjDiddles: Smiley, I'll kick your ass, you little punk!

Smiley: Yeah, I know you got that courage dot com. You try talking to me like that to my face, bitch!

coutorture
Tortured by fashion.

Girl, those hot-pink rabbit-fur zebra hot-pants are just plain coutorture on my eyes!

cowboy up
When things are getting tough and you have to get back up, dust yourself off, and keep trying.

Let's all cowboy up and get this job finished!

coworked
When you are doing something at work that is not work-related that requires your full attention, such as playing a video game, and a coworker suddenly pops in, forcing you to make it look as if you are busy and hide your game (such as with alt-tab). After the coworker leaves, you typically return to your video game to find your character dead.

Joe: Hey, man, what are you doing? Are you gonna help us capture the flag?

Bob: Sorry, I got coworked! Had to alt-tab!

crackalackin'

Happening. A way of saying "How are you doing?" used by soda-drunk junior-high kids being their usual crazy selves.

Yo, Sabrina, what's crackalackin'?

crack a rim

To act foolishly or recklessly with a vehicle, usually under the influence of one or more mind-altering substances, to the point of damaging the vehicle.

Shortly after drinking at home, Kyle and Jared couldn't even make it out of the neighborhood without cracking a rim.

crackberry

Nickname for the popular RIM Communications device BlackBerry. The device is a phone, PDA, and email appliance. Users/owners are typically addicted to checking email and swapping short messages on the device. They are as addicted as a crackhead is to the pipe.

Look at him. Like he's a pimp/playuh all hooked up on his crackberry.

crack TV

Television show you watch when you're high—not high from crack specifically, but from any substance, or even drunk.

Me and Mike was watching crack TV after the cookup session—hours of Spongebob Squarepants, Looney Tunes, local programming, and infomercials.

craptastic

When something both sucks and blows; when "fantastic" just can't be said ironically enough.

Have you seen the new reality TV show? Man, it's totally craptastic!

C.R.E.A.M.

Money. Acronym for "cash rules everything around me." Used by the Wu-Tang Clan on *Enter the Wu-Tang (36 Chambers)*.

As much as I know C.R.E.A.M., I am still an idealist.

credit whore

Someone who does something nice just so they can bring it to everyone's attention and get credit for it.

A credit whore is someone who puts money in a tip jar and then shouts, "I just put a dollar in the tip jar."

creeping

Banging someone while you're taken.

Shaggy's girlfriend caught him red-handed creepin' with the girl next door.

crib

Home, domicile, or dwelling.

Dang du . . . your crib is phat, yo! (Translation: Your house is very pleasing to the eye; it has contemporary flair yet is structurally sound. May I have a look around, my good man?)

critical ass

The stage in fat accumulation when fabric can no longer contain the enormity of one's buttocks.

Jesus, I can't zip up these jeans anymore— I've reached critical ass!

crooked letter

The letter "s."

I'm rolling through the M-I-crooked letter-crooked letter-I tonight.

cropdust

To fart, then drag the smell around with you, or fart while walking. One who does this is called a "cropduster."

Wes decided to cropdust the entire back half of the apartment, so he walked from the laundry room through the living room into the bedroom, all the while farting and pulling the smell with him.

crosstitute

A person, usually of the hardcore religious right, who uses the word of God to further a political agenda; similar to a "fundie," e.g., Pat Robertson, Jerry Falwell, George W. Bush, etc.

Randall Terry was on TV last night crosstituting for Terri Schiavo.

crotchfruit

Derogatory term for a child.

I really hate summer. My town is full of crotchfruit all the time, since they don't have to be in school then.

crotchular

A description of one's genital region; most commonly used in conjunction with the word "region."

Mike's fist struck Steve's crotchular region after Steve asked Mike, "What are you doing with your life that's so impressive?"

crowdway

A path through a crowd at parties. One should use crowdways to go from point A to point B to annoy the least possible amount of people.

We need to find a crowdway to get to the nearest bar.

cruise control

When you are detached from the world; you glide through, paying limited or no attention to events that occur around you. You often stare into space. You may daydream, but most of the time you aren't really thinking about anything. You may feel lost, even in familiar surroundings. This can result from the breakup of a relationship, trouble within the family, or the death of someone close to you. It may involve drug use.

Ever since my cat died, I've been totally out of it. I'm on cruise control.

cruiser spoon

To park two police cruisers with the driver's sides adjacent so that the officers can converse through the open windows.

Better slow down, the po-po are cruiser spooning in the parking lot ahead.

crunchy

Quasi-modern-day hippie; tends to wear no shoes, spends much of his time finding his way out of the woods after smoking excessive amounts of weed, favors the fragrance of patchouli.

Does it smell like feet in here? Oh yeah, it's that crunchy kid having found his way out of the forest.

crunk

Crazy drunk. Severe intoxication or getting drunk; a very fun or enjoyable time; also used to describe something cool, hip, or fashionable.

Yo, I'm on my eighth shot . . . this party is crunk!

crymax

To sob in gratitude after sex.

I totally crymaxed after I tapped that ass.

cu

"See you."

omg i cu later kthxbye

cube cruising

Spending a significant portion of the work day visiting cubes and chit-chatting about any and every thing. Cube cruisers either have too little work to do, or they simply don't care if their low productivity causes a bottleneck in the office.

Jill began her cube-cruising circuit at approximately 8:15 every morning.

cubicle speed

Caffeine-laden food/drugs used to stay awake in a modern office environment.

Coffee, caffeinated tea, Xenadrine pills, caffeine pills, Starbucks lattes—what's your favorite cubicle speed?

cubular

Anything that is "cool" in a "business-geek" office context; often used ironically. This is a term derived from "cubicle" and the surf-slang "tubular."

The latest BlackBerry, a new flat-panel display, highly effective CRM software, an entertaining web site, the latest designer cubicle-space or office furniture: All these things are cubular.

cush

A special form of hydroponic marijuana; very powerful with long-lasting effects.

What do you wanna smoke? The nugs of chronic, or some bomb-ass nugs of cush?

cut eye

To glare at someone with such angry ferocity that your eyes become little more than slits.

That girl on the merry-go-round gave you some cut eye!

c-wrap

A condom.

Yo, Lonnie, hook me up with a c-wrap.

cyber

Online sex that loners engage in if they are too ugly and boring to get a real boyfriend/girlfriend.

Loner 1: Hey wanna cyber?

Loner 2: Sure, baby, let me virtually take my clothes off.

cyberchondriac

When one becomes so obsessed with medical web sites on the Internet that they diagnose themselves with certain illnesses that more often then not they don't have, thus making the situation worse.

My cyberchondriac episode in May left me with thousands in unnecessary medical fees.

cyber Monday

Cyber Monday is the Monday after Black Friday, when online retailers make their biggest sales to customers who saw products over the Thanksgiving weekend, and will now be ordering them Monday at work.

Forget those long Black Friday lines. I'm going to order on Cyber Monday!

C

dictionary

D

daggy

Australian slang for not stylish, out of fashion, not trendy, uncool, untidy, unclean, not neat.

That outfit makes you look daggy.

damn skippy

Not just yes, but *hell* yes.

Police officer: Did you shoot the man who accosted your girlfriend?

Suspect: Damn skippy. And I'd shoot him again if I had another bullet.

dance boner

A spontaneous erection generated by friction from vigorous, shameless grinding.

I totally popped a dance boner last night when I was grinding on Jenny.

dancing with the train

The destruction or ruin of one's own interests; committing suicide; an unequivocally crazy-assed "this will end it" choice.

Dude, if you tell your boss to go to hell you are dancing with the train.

dark business

When two people hate each other for no reason other than to hate each other, or when people talk behind each other's backs, or when people get in stupid fights just to get into a stupid fight. Drama.

Mike: Why does Charlie hate you so much?

Jim: Just some stupid dark business.

darkspeed

Really slow; opposite of lightspeed.

Way to go darkspeed. Could you go any slower?

dark-thirty

The thirty minutes before or after nightfall.

I told David the party starts at dark-thirty.

date hair

Hair that is commonly slicked with a greasy additive and parted in the middle with the hair curling at the end. Used to impress a date or when one is attired in one's "Sunday best."

Damn, Joey. That date hair looks like Ricky Ricardo had sex with a wet rat.

date shield

A female friend who shows no outward interest in you, but will go all out to prevent you from hooking up with other women by slagging you behind your back.

I was so ready to hook up with Sheila, but Annie date-shielded me.

daytime playtime

The ability to hook up with a sex partner during normal business hours.

Hey, baby, why don't we have some daytime playtime!

dayum

An exclamatory word, not unlike "Whoa!" It is a more emphasized version of the word "damn" when it is used in the same way.

Dayum! Your sister's hot!

d bag

Short for "douche bag"; someone who is socially dysfunctional in some way. Generally an asshole; someone who does something shady and low to someone else.

Mike: Hey, Mal, talk to Jason lately? He never calls me back.

Mal: What a d bag.

DDF

Acronym for "drug- and disease-free." Often found in online personals ads, especially for casual sex.

I am 24, 5'10", size 6, pretty, fun, nonsmoker, social drinker, love to laugh. I'm looking for a man to play with. Age and weight are not important, just be taller than me, funny, and DDF.

dead babies

Bad luck, mishaps, bad circumstances.

After the boat started taking in water, they knew it was all dead babies from here on out.

dead drop

A location used to secretly pass items between two people, such as spies or drug dealers, without requiring them to meet. A common technique is to duct-tape the item to the underside of a toilet cover in a public restroom. A signal, like a pile of stones in a certain formation, is sometimes used to indicate there is something to pick up. After the drop is checked, the signal is removed.

The dead drop is the restroom toilet at the Gulf station at the corner of Commercial Avenue and Georges Road.

dead it
To end something, such as a relationship.

Man, that girl is crazy! You need to dead it!

dead zone
Any geographical area that lacks cell phone service or has very poor reception.

I should not have signed up for my provider because their service sucks shit on the East Coast. They have so many dead zones in their so-called coverage area.

death breath
When your friend says hello and you fall back two paces, he has death breath.

Where did you eat last night, in a grave-yard?! Damn, that's some death breath!

debo
To steal or take away from.

That SOB just deboed my car!

decidership
A form of government in which one person, who regularly disregards opinions, petitions, and mandates of the people and elected representa-

tives, exercises absolute power and unrestricted control.

The misguided war on terrorism has turned the USA from a democracy to a decidership.

deep
The number of people who were at a location.

The party was at least fifty deep.

deets
Details. Usually pertains to gossip.

My friend wanted to know what happened at the party last night, so I gave her the deets.

defo
Definitely; for sure.

Manny: Do you like Louisa?

Ty: Defo!

deja booty
Randomly bumping into someone you have slept with before and retapping that ass.

My friend scolded me for my recent encoun-ter with some deja booty.

delish
Delicious.

That was delish. Can I have more?

de-loosify
Loosen.

Slim Bavis made the big switch to Tropicana from Minute Maid orange juice because he was unable to de-loosify the lid.

denglish

A term used by linguists, mainly based in Germany, to describe incorrect English as spoken by Germans whose sole contact with English is at school. Examples of denglish:

Body bag: a fashionable bag worn over the shoulder

Last, not least: last, but not least

dental denial

To use mouthwash instead of brushing one's teeth before going out for lack of time or total laziness.

I put on some deodorant and did a dental denial but still got to work ten minutes late.

depantsification

1. Having one's pants removed.

Paul walked in the room to see Andrew in a state of depantsification.

2. Losing one's authority in a household; no longer wearing the pants.

After always allowing his girlfriend to have her way, Sam knew that he had succumbed to depantsification.

derection

What a guy gets when he looks at somebody really ugly.

Guy 1: Ew, dudes, look at that fugly chick over there!

Guy 2: Ahhh! My eyes!

Guy 3: Ahhh! My derection!

desend

To take back something, such as an email or letter.

Man, I really bitched her out in that email; I wish I could desend it!

designer stubble

Remnants of facial hair that create a dark area around the mouth area. Designer stubble is fitting only on certain men, making them look rough yet attractive. Not a good look on women.

He's tall, dark, and handsome, with designer stubble!

designer water

A commercial brand of mineral water, often served or sold under pretentious circumstances or marketing and/or at exorbitant cost.

I went to the cocktail bar with the guys, but since I was drivin' I had to sip designer water all evening.

deuces

1. Holding two fingers up in the gesture of the "peace" sign.

On the way out of the door, he threw those deuces up and said, "I'll check you all later."

2. Verbal expression similar to "peace" or "peace out." taken from the hand signal that means "peace."

I'm outta here, man. See you later. Deuces.

devil horns

The hand gesture made by metal heads when hearing music they like. Made by holding the middle and ring finger down with the thumb while holding index finger and pinky straight.

I don't need many beers in me before I start flashing the devil horns.

devil music

Music that an older or religious person finds offensive, unholy, or just plain stupid.

MTV plays nothing but devil music anymore . . . nothing with moral values.

devil's fork

Deviation from steady stream flow of urine, in which the piss takes two independent paths, one of which is usually outside the porcelain bowl and often directly on the trouser leg or shoe. Includes "devil's forking," in which both feet get a hosing, and "devil's fork special," a game in which one attempts to secure flow into two urinals simultaneously.

I impressed the lads in the gents by a spectacular display of devil's forking, in which I simultaneously pissed on the legs of the persons to the left and right of me.

dial while intoxicated (DWI)

When you get high on any substance, but usually alcohol, and set the record straight with exes, family, coworkers, former teachers, etc.

I dialed while intoxicated and called my best friend from first grade. We decided to join the Marines.

dick move

An action by one male to a male friend that violates understood social expectations, especially where the transgressor obtains a slight advantage in comparison to a relatively large inconvenience imposed upon the aggrieved party.

Tom and Bill were both interested in the same girl at the bar; when Tom insinuated that Bill had erectile dysfunction, that was a dick move.

dick trap

When a woman asks a man a question and no matter how he answers or which choice he makes, he is in trouble.

Girlfriend: Can I see your porn collection, honey? I promise I won't get mad.

dictionary.com

The suburban dictionary.

Golly gee, Mr. Wilson, I need to go look that up on dictionary.com. For sure!

digisexual

An individual who surrounds him/herself with high-tech toys and gadgets to compensate for a lack of flesh-to-flesh interaction.

Ron: Yo, dawg, let's go to the mall and pick up some hoes.

Leo: Got no time for hoes. Can't you see I'm playing the PSP?

Ron: Damn, since when did your bitch ass turn digisexual?

digitard

Anyone who has difficulty using technology for even the most basic of tasks, such as making a call on a cell phone.

My eighty-year-old grandma is such a digitard, she actually thought she could play the .m4a files she downloaded from iTunes on her Dell DJ.

Dilbert

An office loser. Any office employee who embodies some characteristics of the main character in the comic strip *Dilbert*, created by Scott Adams, which depicts employees who work in cubicles for a clueless boss at a large company.

The young Dilbert tried in vain to sell his boss on the new technology, but his boss told him to shut up and consider himself lucky he even has a Coleco.

dime piece

A girl who is bangin', hot, beautiful, a perfect ten.

Jess is a dime piece, bro.

dine and dash

Going into a restaurant, sitting at a table, ordering whatever you want, eating, and then leaving quickly without paying.

Yesterday I went to this fancy-ass restaurant, ordered a $200 meal with the best wine out there, and when the waitress turned around I left in a second! Ha ha ha!

dingleberry

A small piece of poo clinging for dear life on the ass hair like it's the gym rope.

Ahhh, a dingleberry! Where are the scissors?

DINK

Acronym for "dual income, no kids."

Me and the missus are DINKs, so we don't have any kids to spend the money on.

dinner whore

A girl who is exclusively after a free meal or an expensive gift. She actively seeks out dates with well-off men who will wine and dine her at upscale restaurants. She is usually physically attractive enough to make the man fall for her feminine wiles. She will rarely have sex with these men until they spend a certain number of dollars on her. Nobody knows exactly what that number is, so the man keeps spending and spending, while the dinner whore keeps living it up.

As a mere graduate student living on a stipend, it is impossible to find a date in New York, which is saturated with dinner whores.

dip

1. To leave abruptly. To get the hell out of somewhere.

When I saw the Vanilla Ice CD in my date's CD player, I knew I had to dip.

2. To hit the gas and then brake, causing your car to rock back and forth.

We dippin' in the '64.

Dirty Third

A synonym for the Dirty South; derived from the terms "Dirty South" and "Third Coast."

This ain't New York. This ain't L.A. This is the Dirty Third.

discolocate

To break or harm one's limbs or organs through dancing.

Jeff discolocated his knee with his wack dance moves.

disco nap

Sleeping when you have something goin' on later that you need to get ready for.

I was about to go to the club, but I needed a disco nap to feel refreshed.

dish jenga

The pile of precariously balanced dishes in a dish rack that cannot be disturbed lest there be an avalanche of china, crockery, and silverware.

Don't touch the dish jenga! That's a load-bearing spoon.

DISH JENGA

Dish jenga is closely related to "tetrising it"—fitting a lot of stuff into a small space, like a suitcase or a small trunk. You always knew those Tetris skills you spent hours building would come in handy.

ud

Disneyfied

Something that has been sanitized in order to project the sanctity of family values.

I hate Las Vegas. It's become so Disneyfied.

djeetyet

Slang for the phrase, "Did you eat yet?"

Mark says, "Djeetyet?" and Frank replies, "No, ju?"

DL

Acronym for "down low," as in "Keep it on the down low," i.e., keep it quiet; mum's the word.

I got that on the DL, so don't be broad-casting it.

doctor shopping

Alternating doctors to obtain overlapping prescriptions. Most commonly done to obtain painkillers such as OxyContin.

The USA's highest-rated radio host, Rush Limbaugh, was accused of doctor shopping to obtain thousands of OxyContin pills once he became addicted to them.

dog beers

Measurement used when an individual brags about the amount of beers consumed in a given night; to measure your beer count in dog years, i.e., times seven.

Jim: I drank thirty-five beers last night.

Mike: Dog beers, maybe.

dom

Short for "dominant"; the dominant person in a BDSM relationship or encounter.

She's looking for a dom who has knowledge of tying complicated knots.

The Donald

Nickname for entrepreneur Donald Trump; as used on NBC's *The Apprentice.*

Well, looks like The Donald has fired someone again tonight.

donions

1. Done, finished, complete.

Person 1: Hey, man, you have any more exams this week?

Person 2: Hell no, man, I'm donions.

2. Wasted; intoxicated from drugs and/or alcohol to the point at which no more partying shall take place for the evening/morning.

Wow, look at that kid passed out on the couch. He's donions. . . . Hey, hand me that marker!

3. In over one's head; in a great deal of trouble; screwed.

When her father came home early from work and found us in bed, I was donions.

Don't drop the soap!

A remark made to someone being hauled off to jail, particularly someone you dislike. Implies that once in jail, if the person drops a bar of soap in the shower, he will be forced to bend over and retrieve it.

"Don't drop the soap!" I yelled as the burglar was taken away by the police from my home. His eyes began to tear up as he anticipated that hot, steamy shower.

Don't hate the player; hate the game.

Do not fault the successful participant in a flawed system; try instead to discern and rebuke that aspect of its organization that allows or encourages the behavior that has provoked your displeasure.

Teacher: You have plagiarized this essay.

Student: Don't hate the player; hate the game.

Doogie Howser

Coined from the '80s TV show of the same name, a "Doogie Howser" is a kid with a genius-level IQ who excels in all academics and is smarter than their peers.

Phil: Hey, Steve, it's Friday night! You wanna party?

Steve: No, I need to stay in and study. I have that calculus exam in a week, and I need to prepare myself.

Phil: OK, Doogie Howser. Have fun nerding it up!

doorknob

An easy girl who sleeps around; so called because everyone gets a turn.

Yo, that chick is a doorknob; don't wife that.

doorbuster

An eye-popping sale that only runs for a short period of time on Black Friday. These sales are used to draw people into stores early on, and they usually result in long lines of people waiting for stores to open.

See that long line of people waiting outside Best Buy, Edmund? It ain't for free soup. There's probably a doorbuster there.

doored

To crash into a driver's side door of a vehicle while riding your bike. A painful biking experience in which two conflicting worldviews collide.

Biker 1: What happened to your face?!

Biker 2: I was riding down First and some asshole yuppie got out of their beemer without looking, and I got doored and did a face-plant.

dork walk

A form of walking characterized by an exaggerated stride and arm swing, usually performed by white suburban women wearing headphones and athletic attire. Since it isn't really strenuous, the dramatic motions and attire lets observers know they are exercising, not just too poor to afford a car.

Check that out that dork walker—she must work at the Ministry of Silly Walks.

dose
A hit of acid; LSD.

Can I get some doses?

double bagger
A woman so ugly that having sex with her is only possible with the use of two bags: one over her head, and a second bag over your own head in case her bag falls off.

Kelvin's mom is a double bagger.

double dip
Favorite behavior of crude diners. Involves dipping your crudités or corn chip into a sauce, taking a bite from the veggie or chip, and then redipping the half-digested item back into the sauce. Made famous on *Seinfeld* some years back.

Sign at county fair food stall: DO NOT DOUBLE DIP!

double exposure
An Internet dating term. When a person you are meeting for the first time is wearing the same outfit pictured in their Internet dating profile.

On the date Mike realized a double exposure had occurred when Jennifer wore the same blue sweater pictured in her Match.com profile page.

double nickel
Fifty-five miles per hour.

The speed limit through town is double nickel.

downchuck
The opposite of upchucking. When you vomit a bit, and you accidentally swallow it. Leaves a nasty taste in your mouth and can often happen many times if you are hungover.

Damn it, after that massive party I down-chucked like eight times.

drain the lizard
To take a piss (males).

Dude, pull over, I need to drain the lizard.

dramarama
A situation in which one or more individuals choose to take a relatively benign event and turn it into a huge drama.

Don't drag me into your current drama-rama, missy!

drama trap
A scheme engineered by a drama lover to suck a victim into a situation or succession of events in real life that has the dramatic progression or emotional effects characteristic of a play.

Jessica encounters Billy, a potential sexual partner. She does not know if Billy is interested in her. Jessica tells all of her friends about Billy, exaggerating her feelings for him and even creating made-up facts. She is setting up a drama trap by entangling her friends into this situation. Whether Billy rejects her or likes her back doesn't matter, because each scenario will provide Jessica grounds for intense drama within her group of friends.

drippin' stains

A clean-looking clear coat on a paint job that makes the car appear wet.

My caddy is an SLS drippin' stains with black paint.

drive-by

When your boss or coworker stops by your desk to talk to you about things instead of scheduling a meeting with you, especially when that boss or coworker interrupts a meeting you're already having with someone else.

Norman got a drive-by from the CEO while we were having our weekly meeting, and now we have two more projects to complete by the end of the year.

driver's arm

A left arm that is tanner (or redder) than the right arm because it's been hanging out the window.

Dude 1: Hey, man, I took a trip to L.A. last weekend.

Dude 2: Yeah, man, I know. You've got major driver's arm!

drive the Bronco

To be an accomplice or accessory to an act. A reference to A. C. Cowlings driving O.J. Simpson on a nationally televised slow-speed freeway chase after the murders of Nicole Brown Simpson and Ron Goldman.

Guy 1: Did you get your little brother drunk at that underage party?

Guy 2: Naw, but I guess I was driving the Bronco since I told him about it.

drive the bus

To unintentionally drive a common route. To turn on the mental auto-pilot and drive toward a location other than your desired destination. For example, you set out to drive to the store, but after a few minutes find that you are halfway to work.

If I'm not careful, I end up driving the bus to work on Saturday mornings.

drive the porcelain bus

To have too much to drink and wind up with two hands on the opened toilet in a kneeling position puking your guts out.

Man, am I exhausted! I drank too much and was driving the porcelain bus all night!

driveway jewelry

A highly expensive car or motorcycle

that's been left to sit in the driveway, unused. Much like a flashy diamond ring or gold necklace, its sole purpose is to demonstrate wealth.

That's a $45,000 bike in his driveway with only a hundred miles on it. Clearly, he bought it for driveway jewelry and bragging rights.

drop

1. To knock someone to the ground.

He was stepping up, thinking he was king shit, so I dropped that little bitch.

2. To shoot/kill someone.

We should drop that mofo before shit gets outta control.

3. To take Ecstasy orally.

I dropped two pills an hour ago and I'm tripping balls!

4. To release an album to the public.

The new Jay-Z dropped last week.

droplift

The opposite of shoplifting. To leave a product or item in a shop, rather than take one. It has been used by artists and musicians to promote their work for free, while some people use droplifting to make political or economic statements (for example, by altering a shop's products and then returning them).

Guerrilla artist Banksy droplifted doctored copies of Paris Hilton's debut album in record stores in the UK. He changed the

cover art and included his own remixes, titled "Why Am I Famous?" "What Have I Done?" and "What Am I For?"

drop paper

To submit a résumé to employers, particularly when trying desperately to escape a sinking ship.

The entire development team at Living.com started dropping paper the day after it showed up on fuckedcompany.com.

drop screens

To screen phone calls. Deliberately not answering because you don't want to talk to a particular person.

Rick isn't answering his phone, he's droppin' screens.

drop trou

To lower one's pants to one's ankles, often in a sudden, impulsive manner, thus exposing one's nether regions.

We all dropped trou and mooned the old lady.

drugstore cowboy

A poseur who dresses up as a cowboy to do noncowboy activities.

Todd only dresses up as a cowboy when he goes clubbing. He is a drugstore cowboy.

drunk catcher

An obstacle in one's path that, when one is drunk, provides an incredible challenge to avoid. Includes cracks in the sidewalk, low-hanging tree branches, abnormal curbs, and members of the opposite sex who are of questionable attractiveness. Generally, drunk catchers are ranked by class or degree of difficulty; class 1 is the lowest difficulty and class 5 is the highest.

The captain totally tweaked his ankle last night on a class 5 drunk catcher.

Daylight saving time–lag came a month early for Americans in 2007, because of a law signed by President Bush as part of a new energy plan. According to Reuters, utility companies reported no measurable impact—but the real question is, did Starbucks sell more Frappuccinos to the DST-lagged on the following Monday?

DST-LAG

drunk MySpace

Much like the drunk dial or the drunk text, it is contacting someone by way of your MySpace account while sloppy drunk and sending messages and/or comments that you will most likely regret once you sober up. Also: "drunkspacing."

Jane: What are you doing getting back together with Mike? I thought you had a restraining order against him.

Andrea: What are you talking about?

Jane: Yeah, girl, you left him a comment last night that says you love him and he's the one for you—it's right here on his MySpace page.

Andrea: Oh my God, I drunk MySpaced Mike last night! I didn't mean that!

DST-lag

The jetlag-like disruption of your circadian rhythms that occurs on the Monday after daylight saving time comes into effect.

Sorry I'm late. I've got the goddamn DST-lag. It took three cups of coffee before I could wake up enough to leave the house.

dudess

The female version of dude, according to George W. Bush.

In a White House ceremony last night, President Bush said hello to the "dudes and dudesses" from the U.S. Winter Olympics Team.

Next time you're drunk MySpaceing, leave a comment on Urban Dictionary's MySpace: myspace.com/urbanup.

DRUNK MYSPACE

dumb smart

Someone who thinks they know a lot, and tries to talk like they're smart, but when engaging in debates, they never prove their point.

Fundo thought he was engaging in intel-lectual conversation with the smartest lady in the world, until he found out she was only dumb smart.

dumb stupid

Crazy, retarded, slow.

He was bombing on you and you was up there looking dumb stupid.

dumpee

The loser in a relationship that is being dumped.

Jenny was devastated that she was dumped by her boyfriend, making her the dumpee.

dunzo

Done, finished. Used by the *Laguna Beach* cast.

This car is so dunzo.

dupe

1. A duplicate.

There are too many dupes on urbandictionary.com.

2. To duplicate something.

The idiot was bored so he duped someone else's definition and added some offensive words.

3. To deliberately confuse or scam someone.

The idiot was easily duped out of his cash.

dustache

A faint, almost imperceptible mus-tache usually found on adolescent boys and some women.

He rocks his dustache and listens to Primus.

dutchie

A joint made from a Dutch Master cigar.

Pass the dutchie on the left-hand side and fix that canoe.

dutty

Literally "dirty" pronounced with a West Indian accent. Can also have a positive connotation, for example Sean Paul's album title *Dutty Rock*.

The girl is pretty, but she is corrupt and dutty!

In a positive usage: Booya! That freestyle was dutty!

DWHUA

Acronym for "driving with head up ass."

We didn't drink in high school, but we did DWHUA often.

DYJGTIY

Acronym for "Did you just get the Internet yesterday?"

Honestly, DYJGTIY?

dyke tyke

A guy that likes to hang around les-bians. A male version of a fag hag.

Most of Harry's friends are lesbians, but he isn't trying to get any action. I think he's a dyke tyke.

E

ear candy
Something (music, a person's voice) particularly pleasing to the ear.

Snoop Dogg is ear candy.

eargasm
The sensation one gets while hearing a dramatic climax in music.

I nearly had an eargasm while listening to his performance of Rachmaninoff's Piano Concerto No. 2.

earjacking
Eavesdropping on a conversation that you have no business hearing.

Bob totally earjacked my conversation with Susie and now everyone knows I got a boob job.

earlate
Anywhere between the hours of 4 a.m. and 7 a.m. When you've been up all night and it's getting late, but technically it's early. The mixture of early and late.

I looked at the clock, and it was 5 a.m. It sure is earlate.

earmuffs
A command directed toward a child so he will cover his ears while an adult curses.

Earmuffs, Billy. Earmuffs.

Earth
God's reality TV show.

That planet gets good ratings on Uranus.

eat babies
Something done when one is bored and doesn't really feel like cooking.

Man, I got so fried I ate babies.

e-bandon

To suddenly stop emailing someone (friend/business associate) after correspondence has already been established.

I bumped into an old college friend and we emailed for while, but when I suggested getting together she e-bandoned me.

eBayonet

To suffer an unfortunate turn of events on the online trading community eBay. Often involves bidding for items one does not really want, being caught up in bidding wars, and being tricked into bidding for faulty or false items.

When the life-size cardboard cutout of George Clooney I purchased for $100 arrived in the mail, it became apparent that I had been eBayoneted.

e-bortion

When someone starts an Internet activity (e.g., MySpace or making a web page) only to give it up in a period of two to three weeks.

I made a MySpace account the other week but I had to have an e-bortion because I actually have a real life.

e-burn

A slap in the face via the Internet.

An e-burn includes, but is not limited to, deletion from a MySpace friends list,
deletion from a buddy list, getting blocked, or failing to receive e-props or kudos on a blog.

e-condom

A term used for all Internet security (firewalls, antivirus, antispam, etc.). All computers should have an e-condom.

Don't let your computer get ITDs; wrap it up with an e-condom!

economy triple

An economy triple is a room in a dormitory supplied by a school, in which three people are thrust into a room intended for two people for the sake of paying less. Truth be told, there is nothing economical about squeezing three people into a two-person room. Nothing.

You'll find that intrinsic values of privacy far outweigh the money saved by opting for an economy triple.

eco porn

A corporate advertisement that extols the company's environmental record or policies, usually by a company known to rape and pillage the environment as often as possible.

Abe: Have you seen those new commercials by the oil companies that show how good they are for the environment?

Babe: They are pure eco porn, man.

e-crush

A crush on someone you met on the Internet.

Stop having an e-crush! Get someone who's 100 percent not a fake person!

EDM

Acronym for "electronic dance music." Includes trance, house, techno, breakbeat, gabber, hardcore, and much, much more.

I like EDM in general—not just trance.

e-dump

To ditch someone via email, IM, or text message. Usually done because the e-dumper does not have the balls to tell the e-dumpee to his or her face that he or she is dumped.

I was chatting with this chick I met on the Internet for a couple weeks, then she e-dumped me for someone she met in real life.

effed in the a

A different way of saying, "Dude, we're screwed."

If we get caught, we're gonna be effed in the a!

effuculate

To mess up massively via an electronic medium.

I've just effuculated by sending an email to my friend saying "My boss is an asshole," and accidentally copying my boss.

ego wall

A wall, usually in a professional's office, covered with an inordinate number of framed diplomas, certificates, and other tokens of academic achievement. The sheer number of items implicitly speaks to the superior skill or intelligence of the professional who earned them. This outward display mirrors and reinforces the professional's perception of self, or ego.

The lawyer's clients more easily parted with their money upon seeing the ego wall in his office.

> **EGO WALL**
> The "ego wall" is closely related to the "ego search." Maybe your Google ego search results are your ego wall of the digital age.

e-hole

A person who sends useless mass emails—usually jokes or chain letters.

Look, more crap from that e-hole. He's screwing up my machine.

eight ball corner pocket

A way of saying, "I am done with this situation and you." Confident in the fact that you are done, as you would be in making a corner shot in a pool game.

Eight ball corner pocket, dude. Later!

e-lationship

When a couple (friends, lovers, whatever) meets and communicates only via online correspondence (email, IM chats, video rooms, etc.).

Alex: Jasmine and I have a great e-lationship, dude.

Bud: Um, she lives in Vietnam, dude.

Alex: I know, but she writes very flirty emails. And her MySpace is totally hot.

eldercut

When an older member of the human race doesn't feel the need to wait in line (usually a buffet of some type) either because their time is running out, or they have given up on any social graces.

My goodness, was that an eldercut? Did that old person just cut in front of me at the buffet line? Well, I guess I will let them get away with it, because they can't hear me anyway.

electile dysfunction (ED)

The state of impotence and abject disinterest toward the political elective process.

Bob: I ain't gonna vote, I can't—got ED.

Tim: ED?

Bob: Electile dysfunction (ED). Had it since Dole ran in 1996.

electrosexual

Someone who chooses video games over sex.

Ryan is a total electrosexual when he chooses Ninja Gaiden over Katie.

elements of hip-hop

The four elements of the late '70s New York City renaissance: bboying (breakdancing), emceeing (rapping), DJing (turntablism), and writing graffiti.

Rap is something you do; hip-hop is something you live.

eleventy billion

A made-up number Keanu Reeves decided to bet for Final Jeopardy on *Saturday Night Live.*

Keanu: I bet eleventy billion dollars.

Alex Trebek: That's not even a real number.

Keanu: Yet!

e-maelstrom

A long and complicated email trail with dozens of CCs discussing a situation almost none of the recipients cares about.

E

Did you get caught in the latest e-maelstrom about the broken widgets?

email paralysis

The inability to send or reply to emails in a timely manner, caused either by their overwhelming number, or an individual's own spineless avoidance of interpersonal communication.

My grandmother's email never received a reply; email paralysis left me ineffectual.

email promotion

When you promote yourself by changing the title in your email signature.

Mike gave himself an email promotion when he changed the title in his email signature from programmer to web manager.

e-maul

An email assault so vicious in tone the recipient loses an eye to you. To e-maul someone is to textually assault an individual via the Internet.

Bennet: Jenny is such a shrew—she tried to get me fired.

John: Let off some steam, Bennet, and send her an anonymous e-maul.

embiggen

A perfectly cromulent word meaning to make bigger.

A noble spirit embiggens the smallest man.

EMAIL PARALYSIS

Severe email paralysis can lead to an "email bankruptcy," when you give up on your email, delete everything, and start over from scratch. But declaring email bankruptcy and ignoring your friends can negatively affect your street cred.

emergency dance party

Used in times of boredom or to break an awkward moment. One simply yells "Emergency dance party!" and counts down from five and starts beatboxing. Everyone there starts dancing for a period of about ten to thirty seconds.

So then I whipped it out . . . cough . . . um, emergency dance party! Five, four, three, two, one!

emo boy

Boys who listen to "you've probably never heard of them" bands, dress with more care and style than most girls, and read in-depth books while sipping on low-fat lattes before they take their Vespas home. Their hair, a special point of interest, is usually styled to look unkempt, jet black, and whooshed over to the side. They are generally tall and thin. They appreciate the arts. They *know* just how much cooler than the rest of us they are.

I know lots and lots of emo boys . . . they took over my favorite café.

emo chick

Girls who rebel against pop culture and say their lives suck. Perpetually attracted to emo guys, with at least one emo ex-boyfriend. Usually have black or red hair that's either long and falls over their face or chin- to shoulder-length with emo bangs. Wear tight black shirts and black jeans or cargos with a lot of black and heavy silver jewelry.

Emo chick: Hot emo guys that can lick their elbows turn me on.

"Emo" is the most-looked-up word—and the word with the most definitions—on urbandictionary.com. Since 1999, people have sent in more than four thousand definitions of "emo." More than one hundred thousand people liked those definitions enough to give them a "thumbs up" on Urban Dictionary.

EMO

ud

emoment

Emo moment. A point in time when an individual engages in whining, complaining, or otherwise self-pitying behavior around others, usually in search of pity.

Jan had a total emoment on her LiveJournal when she started up all that drama about how her boyfriend broke up with her over the Frodo/Aragorn slash forums.

emo stain

E

When an emo kid has a stripe or the front part of his or her hair died a vibrant or contrasting color.

That emo kid Billy is always so sad, and then he got emo stained and it got worse.

emotherapy

A form of rehabilitation of the mind by means of excessive and continuous whining.

I highly recommend you continue your emotherapy.

emoticon

A sequence of printable characters, such as :) or ^_^, that is intended to represent a human facial expression and convey an emotion. Used in Internet forums and instant-messaging.

:) *Smile*

:(*Frown*

;) *Wink*

:P or :fi *Tongue sticking out: joke, sarcasm, or disgusting*

8) *Sunglasses: looking cool*

:O *Surprised*

:S *Confused*

:'(	Shedding a tear
XD	Laughing, eyes shut (LOL)
XP	Tongue out, eyes shut
^_^	Smiley
^.^	See above, but rather than a wide, closed mouth, a small mouth is present
^_~	Wink
>_<	Angry, frustrated
=_=	Bored
-_-	Annoyed
-_-' or ^_^' or ^_^;;	Nervousness, sweat dropping, or embarrassed
¨_¨ or <_<	"Yeah, right," looking around suspiciously
;_;	Crying
o_O	Confused
O_O	Shocked
O_<	Flinch, wink, twitching
._.	Intimidated, sad, ashamed
$_$	Money eyes, thinking about money
x_x	Dead or knocked out
9_9	Eye rolling
_	Starstruck
t(-_-t) or | ,,(-_-),, |	Flipping off
=^_^=	Blushing, or a cat face
u.u	Duh, sarcastic, "What do you think?" face
\m/>_<\m/	Rockin' out

:/	Unsure or sarcastic
:C	The saddest man in the whole entire world
:D	A very happy smiley face
:x	My lips are sealed
\o/	Cheering guy throwing his hands in the air, expressing great happiness
<3	Expression of love
>.<	Frustrated, pissed, upset, or the like
TT	Crying

emotional blackmail

Using fear, obligation, and guilt to manipulate.

Some examples of things emotional blackmailers say: "If you really loved me . . ." "After all I've done for you . . ." "How can you be so selfish?"

employee entrance

The backdoor; anus.

The employee entrance is business only.

empty a leg

Expression used by rough, older British blokes to describe taking a really big piss when they've not been to the bathroom for a while.

Dave—hold on a second. If I don't empty a leg right now I'm gonna piss myself!

end of rhyme

What you say after tearing someone

up in a freestyle rap battle to signify that you have finished verbally bashing them.

Freestyler 1: Man, you suck. You only quack like a duck.

Freestyler 2: Playa, ya rhymes have no grace. Ya betta look out fo' I mace yo face. End of rhyme!

engayed

"Engaged" for gay couples.

Did you hear the news? Paul and Tom got engayed. I can't wait for their wedding!

enlightning

Struck dumb by a revelation of a previously unknown fact. Misspelling of the common word "enlightening" is intentional. Generally used as "struck by enlightning."

When Roy found out that his best friend was gay and had been spying on him in the locker room, he was struck by enlightning.

enron

1. A radical redistribution of wealth, usually from poor to rich; trickle-up theory.

I got enroned, and now I live in a van, down by the river.

2. To be victimized or wronged by the company you work for. The term originated from Enron, a Texas company that collapsed due to corporate scandal, leaving thousands of investors and employees in financial ruin.

We came to work one day and the manager told us the company was closing shop and we could go home. We got enroned with no warning and no severance pay.

enterdrainment

Any passive form of entertainment that is so incredibly mind-numbing that it sucks the intelligence from the listener or viewer.

Sports, celebrity gossip, country music, talk radio, call-in shows, soap operas, and reality TV are considered by many to be enterdrainment.

entremaneur

Someone who makes a living selling bullshit to the masses.

Ted Kennedy certainly is a great entremaneur.

EOD

Acronym for "end of discussion." Used to indicate that, as far as you are concerned, the discussion is over.

For the last time: The sun is yellow, not red. EOD.

e-penis

The technological prowess of an individual (usually within an online or Internet community). Factors that engorge the e-penis include bandwidth, computer speed, hard drive size, and size of DVD collection.

Person A: I have 600GB on my

Alienware and am connected to a T3. My e-penis is huge.

Person B: I share 2GB on my 10-year-old HP and am still on dial-up. Anyone got a tweezers for my e-penis?

epiphanot

An idea that at first seems like an amazing insight (at least to the conceiver) but later turns out to be pointless, mundane, stupid, or incorrect, and often is the root cause of bad decisions. Mostly occurs under the influence of drugs or alcohol.

An epiphanot from the cinematic masterpiece National Lampoon's Animal House:

Larry: OK. That means that our whole solar system could be, like, one tiny atom in the fingernail of some other giant being. (Jennings nods.) This is too much! That means one tiny atom in my fingernail could be—

Jennings: Could be one little tiny universe.

Larry: Could I buy some pot from you?

escape goat

Someone flirted with, obsessed over, and generally courted by a person who's in a relationship they want to get out of.

Jennifer was John's escape goat when he couldn't bring himself to leave Caroline.

e-speak

Any of a variety of different typing techniques used in IM or message boards. Usually hard to comprehend and sometimes unintelligible. In essence, Internet slang and the typing styles that go with it.

Noob: hI GuYS whUts uP. c.o.m.e.o.n g.u.y.s.t.a.l.k t.o.m.e. . . wtf doods i jsut wanna talk 2 u guys

e-stalker

Someone who prowls or sneaks about using online resources to obtain information on someone.

When his ex-girlfriend stopped talking to him, he became an e-stalker and browsed her friend's blog to find out what she was up to.

estrogenda

The secret plot every woman has for her man and the methods she uses to implement it.

My wife wants me to wear a plaid suit. I suspect her estrogenda is to get me to fit in with her Scottish relatives.

e-tact

Tact exercised in an electronic environment, for example, when composing email, instant messaging, or weblogging (or commenting therein).

Jim thought he was being funny and clever, but his comments about my blog lacked e-tact.

e-tard

Someone whose brain is fried from

taking too much E.

Don't roll every weekend or you'll become an e-tard.

evoid

To use technology to avoid human contact.

I saw Jim headed in my direction and evoided him with my iPod.

excessorise

To eat, drink, or take drugs to excess, e.g., drinking a case of beer or eating pounds of meat.

Let's go to the pub and excessorise some tequila.

exersex

To use sex for exercise; to have heated fornication.

Pam: Oh my God. I feel so frustrated . . . and fat.

Rita: Then I suggest you best get out there and get some exersex!

exit interview

The conversation you have with your boyfriend or girlfriend after you break up in which you set boundaries for future communication and discuss how good or bad the relationship was.

My exit interview with my last boyfriend: You suck. Beat it, Corky!

exit strategy

A prearranged plan whereby one leaves an awkward or uncomfortable situation with as much subtlety as possible. Opposite of "walk of shame" when applied to a sexual scenario.

I'm glad I had an exit strategy put in place the next morning. She looked much better with the beer goggles on the night before!

expresshole

A shopper at a store who checks out in the express line when they clearly have more items than the maximum.

Look at this expresshole! He has twenty items when you can only have five in this line!

ex-sex

Sex with an ex. Usually done after a night of heavy drinking. A follow-up of the drunk-dial for a booty call.

A night of ex-sex can lead to a lifetime of hell.

extralegal

Not exactly legal, but still kind of legal . . . in a way.

What my client did was not illegal, it was extralegal. He didn't commit a major crime or anything.

eye bleeder

A video gaming session of preposterous length.

E

I'm not going out tonight. I'm staying in and having an eye bleeder on WoW.

eye booger
Those little green crusties that form on your eyes, most often when you wake up in the morning.

Dude, you've got some major eye boogers. Nasty.

eye rape
To stare at someone for a unnaturally long period of time in a creepy manner. Usually with eyes very wide, or nearly closed with the mouth hanging slightly open. Sometimes accompanied by the licking of lips.

Hey, let's go somewhere else. That guy right there is totally eye raping us.

eye tracks
Imaginary tracks left by the eyes.

The reason so many bookworms wear glasses is to keep from getting eye tracks on their fanzines, magazines, and books.

mo'urban

Facebook dumped

When your significant other breaks up with you and adds insult to injury by declaring him or herself "single" in his or her Facebook/MySpace/Friendster profile.

I'm glad my ex and I never declared our relationship on Facebook. When we broke up at least I didn't get Facebook dumped.

Facebook official

The ultimate definition of a college relationship; one's Facebook profile says "In a Relationship" with your significant other's name.

Brie: Are Adam and Courtney dating?

Tanna: I don't know. They're not Facebook official yet.

face melter

A heavy metal solo that is so awesome and powerful, it causes one's face to melt.

Man, that solo from Master of Puppets is such a face melter.

facepalm

The act of dropping one's face or forehead into one's hand. Usually accompanied by a "thunk" or a cry of "d'oh!" Usually written between asterisks in online conversation, to demonstrate an action.

*Today I locked my keys in my car. Again. *facepalm**

face-turning

Muffling out an interlocutor by slowly yet unexpectedly turning away their head with your hand. Can be construed as either playful or patently insolent by the receiving end.

Randy: You're boring me. (Turns Dina's face.)

Dina: What just happened?

Randy: It's called face-turning, toots. Deal with it.

factory

A paint job, sound system, rims, or anything else that comes standard with a vehicle.

He ain't shit! I got custom candy paint on my car and he ridin' factory!

fagical

Description for something that is utterly gay.

Scott always gets such a fagical look on his face when he sees an 'N Sync video.

fag stag

A heterosexual male who enjoys the company of homosexual males. Benefits of this relationship are social and ego-related improvements for the fag stag, such as fashion advice, social pleasantry train-ing, access to networks of women (mainly fag hags) and matchmaking, complimentary attention from the gay men, and freedom from hetero expectations.

Matt goes to gay bars to find women and his best friends, Brian and Dennis, who are gay.

fagtastic

So fantastically homosexual that it's considered to be one of the most homosexual things on this planet.

Wow, his performance was literally fagtastic.

fagwa

A war declared by gay people on a homophobic person, institution, etc.

Man 1: They threw us out of the party!

Man 2: Well, we'll have to declare a fagwa!

fakester

A profile on Friendster or another social network that is maintained by someone who pretends to be a celebrity or television character but is not.

Hey, man, this Kimmie Gibbler profile is a fakester.

fake-up

A breakup that eventually leads to the couple making back up. Hence, it is not a real breakup, but a "fake-up."

Larry and Susan broke up again, but you know they're going to get back together . . . so it's another fake-up.

fall on the grenade

To make a sacrifice for the good of others. Originally a military term for when a junior officer would deliberately fall to cover a grenade to protect a commanding officer.

Its meaning has been expanded to cover things like taking the blame for a team screw-up (e.g., at work) or humpin' a dawg so your friends can get into the pretty ones.

Always designate a wingman to fall on the grenade!

fansplant

A person with a newly developed appreciation for a sports team; generally acquired after said team has won a championship or become otherwise popular.

Jimmy's uncurved Red Sox hat and Edgar Renteria jersey showed that he was clearly a fansplant; in fact he was from upstate New York.

fantabulous

Sort of like "fabulous" but much more fabulous than the word "fabulous" can convey. Like supercalifragilisticexpialidocious but shorter and easier to spell.

While on a free trip to Italy I won a free titanium-frame bicycle and the Customs agent let me bring it on the plane for free. What a fantabulous trip!

fantathalete

Someone who knows everything there is to know about sports but gets almost no physical activity in his or her life; their main pastime is playing in fantasy sports pools on the Internet.

Normal human being: Dude, wanna go do some midget tossing?

Fantathalete: No way, man, I've got to catch up on my fantasy pools. I've got a draft starting in twenty-five minutes.

Normal human being: Dude, we're playing against hot Las Vegas strippers and they'll be naked.

Fantathalete: Sorry, dude; if I don't start the draft on time the world around me will crumble.

fap

Often used to suggest that something is attractive. The onomatopoeic representation of masturbation.

Did you see those hot pics? Fap, fap, fap!

farmer snort

Plugging one nostril by placing the index finger on it while blowing out the other one in order to discharge nasal mucus onto the ground. The "farmer snort" is a quick, efficient way to blow your nose. Unfortunately, it's also a quick, efficient way to guarantee you won't get a second date, either.

Damn, Frank was pretty glued when he was at Mike's house. First he farted out loud, then he did a farmer snort on the living room carpet. Mike dial toned him on the spot.

fashion victim

A perfectly manicured, groomed, waxed, and buffed person who wears designer-logo clothing but has no real taste or style; wears every faddish trend that comes out.

Paris Hilton is a fashion victim. Someone please arrest her.

fat badge

A stain on your clothing, especially a shirt, resulting from the sloppy eating of greasy food.

After winning the corn-dog eating contest, Carl wore his fat badge with pride, knowing that no detergent known to man would ever remove it.

fat-fingering

Pressing the keys on a cell phone, radio, or computer keyboard and getting improper results because your fingers have hit more than one key at a time. A common problem for those with pudgy fingers, and iPhone owners.

I can't use that cell phone. I keep on fat-fingering the buttons, and I keep on getting wrong numbers!

fat-handed

Being caught in the act of porking out on forbidden food.

I put a ham in the fridge and caught that chunk ass fat-handed eating it.

fathermucker

Less vulgar and more entertaining than the familiar term; "father" is used to confuse the listener. Same methodology as "nucking futs."

It's "nuclear," not "nucular," you stupid fathermucker!

fat jacket

The layer of fat covering the upper body of the average North American. Components include man boobs, back fat, and underarm sag. Although it can be useful in winter, it often hinders mobility, flexibility, and getting laid. Usually made of nachos and cheese or chicken wings, and can be grown thicker through extended periods of sitting on the couch. Requires minimal maintenance, although it must be cleaned often to remove the odor generated by sweat build-up.

The bulkiness of my fat jacket makes it difficult for me to tie my shoes.

fat on the couch

In a very lazy mood. Does not want to get up from the couch or does not want to disturb what they are doing. Also, a lack of excitement that can lead to a buddhalike state of bliss.

mo'urban

Yeah, so the Steelers are on TV and my dad's all fat on the couch, so I don't think I can get a ride out with you.

fattractive

An overweight woman who is, in spite of her girth, considered sexually attractive by a certain group of men, typically whale riders and chubby chasers.

As unattractive as the average man may find them, some men find obese women to be fattractive.

fauxhemian

Conforming to a safe, middle-class lifestyle but with the superficial pretense of an alternative or Bohemian lifestyle.

People who live in Stoke Newington or read the Guardian *may like to believe they maintain the values of their radical student days, but the shallowness of their fauxhemian conceit would quickly be revealed if they were expected to sacrifice some aspect of their comfortable lives.*

fauxlex

Fake expensive watch.

I got this sweet silver and black Submariner fauxlex from the guy at the flea market.

fauxmo/fauxmosexual

A straight man who acts, looks, and dresses as if they're gay in order to appear cool, attractive, or interesting to women.

He's not gay, just a fauxmo.

fauxtography

Staged, doctored, or misleadingly cropped or labeled photographs.

Various bloggers have uncovered several cases of fauxtography in Reuters' photo coverage of the Israel-Hezbollah conflict.

fawkward

Fucking + awkward = fawkward.

I hate hanging out with them; they make me feel fawkward.

f bomb

The strongest weapon in one's verbal arsenal. In a time when words like "bitch" and "ass" have lost their shock value in pop culture, the word "fuck" is still like dropping a bomb in polite conversation.

My teacher called my parents because I dropped the f-bomb in art class.

FCKGW

The first few digits in the serial numbers of many pirated versions of Windows XP, most likely even in your copy.

Those FCKGWing pirates of Windows XP are forcing us to pass on the costs to our legitimate, paying customers.

f'cough

Alternate way of saying "fuck off."

Tit: lol!!! lmao! rofl! thats so kewl dood!

You: F'cough.

fearorism

Government manipulation of the public's fear of terrorism. This tends to be done in order to gloss over recent embarrassment or to push otherwise unpopular bills through the system.

That debate didn't go too well for Bush; he better push the fearorism level up to red tomorrow.

febulights

Christmas lights still present on houses in February.

The neighbors still have not taken down their febulights.

Fed Ex

Kevin Federline's new nickname, since Britney Spears dumped his ass.

What's up, K-Fed, I mean Fed Ex?

The ink was barely dry on Kevin and Britney's divorce papers before this appeared on Urban Dictionary. Within forty-eight hours of their filing, Kevin Federline was handed this special delivery.

FED EX

feeling fist

The fist used to express deep or extreme emotion during a song, in which the singer extends a fisted hand and brings it back in toward their body with intensity of emotion.

When singing "Hungry Eyes" on the karaoke machine, Joe impressed us all with a perfect feeling fist.

feel me?

"Do you understand?"

That cat Jim is weak, feel me?

fem/femme

1. The feminine one in a lesbian relationship.

Ben: Damn, that girl lookin' right.

Dave: Yeah, u right. Too bad she a fem.

2. To men, an insult suggesting they are feminine, gay, a girly-man.

Dude, quit being so fem and get into that strip club!

fembot

A girl or woman who, unfortunately, finds herself oversubscribed to dominant views of beauty and femininity.

Dude, your new stepmom is such a fembot with her plastic surgery, dye job, and falsies. I don't know what your dad sees in her.

fence rider

Someone who takes both sides in a diplomatic confrontation.

He'll never take sides, he's a fence rider!

FFS

Acronym for "for fuck's sake."

FFS, don't include nude pix on your résumé.

fif

To plead the fifth amendment; to not tell something to someone else because of whatever circumstances.

Rick: Tell me what happened last night with that hot chick!

James: Fif.

fifth

A fifth of a gallon of liquor; fifths are sold in bottles containing 750 ml.

Terry was sippin' on his fifth of Taaka.

film

When it's art, you call it a film. When it's mainstream garbage, it's called a movie.

Films: Nosferatu, Triumph of the Will, Citizen Kane, Annie Hall, Raging Bull, The Weather Underground, and Elephant.

Movies: The Fast and the Furious, Titanic, Spider-Man, You Got Served, and Biker Boyz.

fingerfall

The online equivalent of footfall, i.e., the number of people going into online shops.

Fingerfall is up, and this holiday season they're expecting record sales for orders placed on the Internet.

finito

Finished, completed, or gone. In some cases, dead.

When Dad finds out I failed math again, I'll be finito.

fire hazard

A man who is utterly in denial of his homosexuality (in the closet) despite the fact that he is clearly gay to the objective observer (flaming).

Hey, Mike, Jessica's fire hazard of a husband was checking out your ass again.

fist kiss

To punch someone in the mouth.

Anthony wouldn't leave Maggie alone. He wanted to get close to her, but all he got was a fist kiss.

fitch bitch

A girl who wears Abercrombie & Fitch clothing every day of the year.

Check out that fitch bitch over there with her Starbucks latte.

F

dictionary

fivehead

An extremely large forehead.

That girl has a fivehead so big you could show movies on it.

fix yo' weave

A warning said to someone who is getting all up in your face over some trivial matter. Used to indicate that someone is offending your sensibilities or trying your patience. Particularly amusing when said to men with short or no hair. Often followed with "bitch."

You've been on my ass all day about this. Time to fix yo' weave, bitch!

fizzle

A fool; part of the –izzle dialect, in which you take the first letter and add –izzle.

That Nikhil kid, he's such a fizzle.

flag

Head cover representing something (your hood, race, pride, etc.).

Yo, rock that flag again and I'll gat you.

flagaphile

One who is so patriotic they would gladly mate with the American flag.

Stephen Colbert is a flagaphile.

flair

Buttons and other decorative accessories added to a work uniform, especially at chain restaurants. Almost universally despised by restaurant workers and customers alike.

How many pieces of flair are you wearing?

flapjacks

Low-hanging, flat breasts resembling pancakes.

When I was feeling up your grandma, I realized she had mad flapjacks.

flashole

A person who flashes you with their brights even though your brights aren't on.

I was blinded by a flashole going around a corner and ended up in the ditch.

flashpacking

Backpacking but not on a budget, using first-class travel and accommodations. A flashier version of backpacking.

Wow, in-suite bathroom in Budapest. You are good at this flashpacking, aren't you?

flat-ass

True on the most basic level.

I flat-ass couldn't afford a doctor.

flavor of the week

The person you take interest in for one week.

Courtney is Chris's flavor of the week. Last week it was Jessie.

flavor saver

Vertical strip of hair grown underneath the lower lip. A little like a soul patch, but usually more of a strip than a patch.

He's dressed to the nines and sporting a flavor saver.

flexosexual

Someone whose attractions vary.

Today she likes girls, yesterday she liked guys, and who knows how she'll feel tomorrow; she's fairly flexosexual.

flight risk

A person who appears ready to leave a job or relationship, presumably for a better opportunity elsewhere.

Aaron's a definite flight risk. I hear he's posted on Monster.com.

flip a lid

To get mad or upset about something.

My mom would flip a lid if I came home late.

flip it

To sell products or drugs for a profit.

Take this shit to 7th and West and flip it.

flip the script

1. To do the unexpected; to deviate from the norm.

I flipped the script on that bitch when I told her I was leavin' her stank ass.

2. In rap battles, to take what somebody said against you and to use it against them.

When he started hittin' at people I was with that night, I flipped the script by talking about how he didn't even have anyone with him.

flirtationship

When you regularly flirt with an acquaintance or friend but do no more.

Bob has only one girlfriend, but starts a flirtationship with almost every girl he meets.

flist

One's LiveJournal.com friends list.

Dude, I have to check my flist.

floater

1. Fecal matter that refuses to be flushed. Also known as a strong swimmer.

Don't use that stall—there's a floater.

2. A line of bullshit that cannot be accepted.

We didn't believe him, so we said, "That one's a floater."

floordrobe

A form of storage for clothing that requires no hangers, drawers, doors, or effort. Simply drop on the floor and you have a floordrobe.

We have a very stylish Colonial-style his and hers walk-on floordrobe at home.

floorgy

A group of people sleeping on the floor, for lack of suitable sleeping areas. The next morning is characterized by sore backs and necks, complaints about poor quality of sleep, and at least two people hooking up.

We snuck thirteen people into the hotel during the ski trip. The only way we could accommodate them was with a floorgy.

flove

To not merely love something, but fucking love it.

I flove Urban Dictionary.

fluffle

A sign of affection over the Internet. Like you're fluffing a pillow.

He fluffled Kate and skipped off happily.

flush

Having loads of money.

He is flush—look at that mansion.

fly naked

To fly somewhere with the bare-minimum of belongings and purchase the rest where you are.

Man: Aren't you going to pack for New York?

Woman: No, I'm going to fly naked.

FOAD

Acronym for "fuck off and die."

He doesn't like me anymore. He told me to just FOAD.

fojo

Female mojo.

Add some more of that lipstick, girl. We gotta work our fojo tonight.

foley

To make an embarrassing (probably sexual) IM conversation public.

Liz isn't going to school today. She's hiding out because somebody posted her cybers with Todd all over campus—she totally got foleyed.

food baby

When you eat so much your stomach looks pregnant.

Jeez! I ate so much, I look like I am having a food baby!

food coma

The feeling of listlessness, bordering on sleep, that one feels after eating a large meal, often caused by a rush of blood to the stomach and intestines during food digestion.

Man, we ate the whole pupu platter and now I'm slipping into a food coma.

food of shame

Food purchased at a quickie mart or gas station that you take pleasure in eating, but don't admit that you eat.

Jalapeño poppers, Slim Jims, and Red Bull are foods of shame.

food porn

Close-up images of juicy, delicious food in advertisements.

Oh, that McDonald's ad was like food porn. I want a Big Mac sooo bad.

football widow

A woman who must cope with the temporary death of her relationship during football season.

Nothing will draw Stanley away from the TV on Sunday. Jill realized she's become a football widow.

forizzle

For real.

Let's keep it forizzle!

for me to poop on

A phrase used to negate a compliment. Originated by Triumph the Insult Comic Dog.

Me: Hey, that is a good shirt.

You: Really? Thank you!

Me: For me to poop on!

fornever

1. Never occurring, nor having the potential to do so.

Hanson will fornever be the greatest band this country has ever known.

2. A nonexistent period of time.

I could watch Passions fornever and never.

fo' sheezy

Abbreviation of "fo' sheezy my neezy," which is a bastardization of "fo' shizzle my nizzle," which is a bastardization of "fa sho my nigga," which is a bastardization of "for sho mah negro," which is a bastardization of "I concur with you, my African American brother." Used by Snoop Dogg.

Fo' sheezy my neezy.

fo' shindu my Hindu

Like "fo' sheezy my neezy," except for Indian people.

Fo' shindu my Hindu, it's the big neptindu.

foul

1. Really shitty; rotten, spoiled.

That's one foul biatch.

2. Not right, psychologically.

I'm not buying that shit—it's foul!

F

four-wheeling

When you're sitting upright and your head bobs because you're about to fall asleep; it looks like you're driving off-road.

The security guard was fired for four-wheeling at his post.

frag

To kill an enemy in a single-person-shooter computer game.

Dude, my frag count just hit 250. Yeah, man! Unreal Tournament rules!

frankenfood

Food that has been genetically enhanced or has been grown using growth or other hormones.

Hippies often protest over frankenfood.

fratastic

Completely obsessed with one's fraternity.

Wearing his letters to his grandmother's funeral made Dick seem fratastic.

frat rat

A girl who spends exorbitant amounts of time at a frat house, usually with the intent to slut it up with one or more of the fraternity brothers.

Frat guy 1: Man, that chick is over here doing a different brother every week!

Frat guy 2: Yeah, dude. She's a frat rat.

fraudband

A broadband ISP or broadband service that may appear to be of high quality but fails to meet even the lowest of expectations.

wtf? Why won't this stupid YouTube video load? This school has some fraudband, man.

freak flag

Letting loose, being down with your cool self, especially in front of a group of strangers. Your inner freak that wants to come out, but often is suppressed by social anxiety.

Ang: Hey T-Rev, whatcha doin this weekend, bra?

Trev: Ang, I'm gonna fly my freak flag!

freaking

Dancing that simulates sex by grinding the genitalia with suggestive sounds and movements; often done to pop, hip-hop, or rap music.

Freaking isn't allowed at our dances anymore because it offends the chaperones.

free agent

A guy who isn't tied to a single woman; someone with no attachments.

Friend: Yo, that girl is checking you out.

You: All right, dog, I'm going to go over there and let her know I'm a free agent.

freegan

Someone who eats society's wasted food, by scouring the trash for their next meal. Freegans aren't homeless; they just detest society's habit to throw away good food.

As a freegan, Tom would much rather grab bagels out of a bakery's Dumpster than purchase them himself, because he thinks it's a shame how much perfectly good bread gets wasted every day.

free running

A sport and art started in the 1980s in France by bored teenagers, where a person vaults, climbs, and does acrobatic stunts off of objects in their path instead of merely running around them.

The newspaper recently ran an article about a guy who does free running.

free-timer

Like a part-timer or a full-timer, but with no job; someone with a lot of free time.

Kaatisu: So, what do you do during the week?

Girl in club: Oh, I'm a free-timer.

frenemy

Friends, yet enemies. Or an enemy disguised as a friend.

Mark: What do you think about frenemies?

Octavius: I say, keep your friends close, and your frenemies closer.

freshman fifteen

The phenomenon where you put on fifteen pounds in your freshman year.

To avoid the freshman fifteen, you must exercise regularly.

Fridance

A celebratory dance performed on Fridays to commemorate the end of the grueling workweek. The dance is performed using no particular pattern or style, but often incorporates variations of the robot while vocally producing rock or heavy metal type sounds.

My coworker and I did the Fridance in our office several times today.

FREE-TIMER

Also known as "funemployment" or the "after-school special," free-timing is the time in your life when you're unemployed. Maybe unemployment isn't that bad—how else would you have the time to read Urban Dictionary all day?

friend with benefits

A friend with whom you are allowed sexual activity but no true relationship. The benefit is purely sexual and not tied with feelings.

Jane and I are friends with benefits.

front

Put on a fake or false personality; not keeping it real.

He be frontin'—that Benz be a rental!

front burner

An attractive female so hot that she is the large front burner on the stove.

Damn, that hottie is a front burner for sure.

front butt

An enormous, fatty enlargement of the abdomen, genital area, and thigh region that morphs together to create the appearance of a bulbous ass on a person's front.

I saw a woman with a bad case of front butt. It looked as though she had stuffed a pillow down the front of her pants.

fruit fly

An attractive female who hangs around gay males. The same as a "fag hag," but attractive.

Grace is such a fruit fly.

fry tax

When a school lunch table buddy buys a basket of fries, every guy (or gal) within reach of said buddy gets one fry, if and only if they say "Fry tax." If buddy complains about said taxation, whomever he protested to receives one more fry. If it's Friday, or you're just feeling like a jerk, you may state, "Raised taxes!" and may take two or three fries. More than that is just rude.

Mark sits at table with fresh basket of warm, golden school lunch fries.

Mike and Alex: Fry tax!

Mark: What!? NO! Stop!

Mike and Alex: Complaint tax!

Mark: Fine, fine, fine . . .

FUBAR

An acronym for "fucked up beyond all reason." The "r" can also stand for "recognition" or "repair." Often used in the military.

This mission is FUBAR.

f that noise

Another way of saying "no effing way, Jose."

Stupid-ass Kevin said that it would help if I rubbed mayonnaise on my chest. Man, f that noise.

fularious

Intensifier of "hilarious" created by combining "funny" and "hilarious." (You know it's really "fucking hilarious," but if Grandma ever asks . . .)

Everyone was falling off the pews with laughter when Pastor Dave slipped and said Milla was Charles's new ride instead of new bride. It was so fularious, Grandma!

FU money

Any amount of money that allows you to maintain a desired lifestyle without employment or assistance from anyone.

The 6 percent guaranteed interest payments from Bill's investments earn him about $12 million per year. His standard of living requires only approximately $4 million per year. He will never need to be employed by anyone. He has FU money.

funemployment

A happy time in one's life when one is not employed and does not want to be employed.

People wonder how I pay my bills when I'm on funemployment.

funkify

To make something funky.

I funkified the ball with glitter and glow paint.

funky fresh

Really good, swell. New and original.

That new song has a funky fresh beat!

funstroke

A hangover. Anyone who has funstroke is deeply regretting all the daiquiris and lemon-lime Kool-Aid Jell-O shooters the night before. Funstroke may be accompanied by vomiting, headaches, lack of intelligence, or even restlessness or drowsiness.

Oh man, I got so drunk last night, but now I have funstroke and can't stand up.

fun sucker

One who sucks fun. A person who can take any situation in which others are enjoying themselves and remove all pleasure from it.

Bob: Hey, Frank. Wanna go cow tipping with the guys tonight? It'll be a blast!

Frank: My dog was crushed and killed when someone tipped a cow onto him.

Bob: Man, you're such a fun sucker, Frank.

fupa

A woman's fat gut.

Bertha's fupa is bigger than the rest of her body. She's bigger than the fupapotamus; she is a fupasaurus rex.

fur collar

A ring of a man's chest hair around the base of his neck.

Person 1: The guy in the green T-shirt was hot. You could see his fur collar when he was buying stuff at the shop!

Person 2: Ugh, that's gross! I like my men smooth.

furries

A subgroup of science fiction and fantasy fans who focus on cartoon animals, anthropomorphic animals, or human-animal hybrids.

Jody's favorite book is Redwall. *She must be a furry.*

F

Unlike most dictionaries, Urban Dictionary makes no claim to know how to spell a particular word. Urban Dictionary lists at least five different spellings of "fo' shizzle," for example. As a reader, you can choose which spelling fits your fancy by seeing how many people agree with it.

fursona

An artist's representation of him- or herself as a furry.

People are always giving me gift art. Most of the time they draw my fursona for me!

fwisdom

Mindless drivel spoken as if it were fact and backed up with plagiarism and lies.

Christopher is full of fwisdom and it stinks.

mo'urban

game face

That ugly look on your face when you're really into a game.

Damn, that dude right there must be really playing—got his game face on and everything.

gamekiller

A man who interferes with another man's attempt to woo a woman by making him look bad or simply less desirable by comparison.

Woman: I love this club.

Man: Yeah, this song's really good.

Gamekiller: Please, this song sucks. You obviously have no taste. I'm a musician.

gang of

A very large number or amount; a close synonym of "grip of."

A gang of gangs ganged up on my gang in that gang war. Damn, did we get our shit handed to us.

gaper

A beginning skier or snowboarder who has no clue what to do on the mountain. They crash all over the place and get in your way. Referred to as gapers because of the gap between their hat and goggles, aka "gaper-gap."

I couldn't ski fast because I was too busy dodging all the gapers.

gap year

A year off between high school and college.

Taking a gap year is very popular in the U.K.

dictionary

garage racing

Going into your garage to sit on your motorcycle in the off-season.

I put the springer front end on my chopper and did some February garage racing.

garbage time

The closing minutes of a blowout game, when the starters have left and the bench players are playing out the clock. Usually refers to basketball, but can be used in other sports.

Of course Darko scored thirteen points last night. It was in garbage time, dumbass!

gashole

Someone who never offers to help pay for gas, even going out of their way to avoid pitching in.

Jeff is always bumming rides to work but pretends he's asleep whenever I pull into the gas station. What a gashole!

gay bone

Term for a male who is not gay, but exhibits gay tendencies.

Sean has a hot girlfriend and hooks up with a lot of honeyz on the side, but his tight clubwear clothing and love of Gilmore Girls suggests he has a larger-than-average gay bone.

gay card

The figurative membership credential carried by gay men to commemorate the innate knowledge, ability, or sensibility with regard to any subject matter traditionally and generally considered to be the purview of gay men, such as show tunes, color coordination, fashion, hairstyling, interior decoration, or knowing whether any particular man in the vicinity is gay without requiring him to present his gay card.

I haven't seen Rent yet and I can't make quiche, so take away my gay card.

gaydiation

The subatomic beams of gayness emitted by homosexual people.

Tyler emits way more gaydiation than Richard does.

gay for pay

A straight actor who performs homosexual acts in pornographic movies for money.

Sam is gay for pay. He does gay movies then goes home to his wife.

geek bling

Computer parts worn as jewelry. It is generally ostentatious, such as a large network card hanging from a necklace, but it can be subtle as well, like a memory stick on a keychain.

mo'urban

There is also classic geek bling such as bowties and pocket protectors, as everyone knows pocket protectors are the pinnacle of geekdom.

Me: Hey, check out my geek bling. My defcon convention pass from 1999.

Basketball player: That ain't bling, that's just geek.

geek cred
Similar to street cred, but applicable to geeks. Geek cred is allocated by displaying knowledge of different aspects of geek culture such as *Star Wars,* anime, comic books, etc.

You have the unedited original trilogy ripped from the laser discs? That's like, plus-ten geek cred.

geeked
1. Stimulated or energized.

Dude, I am so geeked about U.S. Youth Soccer's National Championships.

2. Mind totally blown from excessive use of an upper (like cocaine or crystal).

Man, I got geeked last night.

geek out
To participate in or talk excessively about a current interest or obsession that is not part of mainstream culture and thus is of little or no importance to an audience.

She told me not to geek out about Capoeira unless I had something new to say.

geek speak
A vernacular of casual English in textual or verbal form, blending verbose, ungrammatical English with technical jargon, 1337/l33t speak, hip-hop lingo, and pop culture quotes/references as an expression of self-referential hip irony among geeks.

W00t w00t! Hollaz to mah Gigga h0mi3z on da Techflizzo' for whose camaraderie and support I am much obliged! All your base are belong to the sysadmin!

gender bender
A function at which the gender roles are reversed or manipulated in various ways. Also, a person who explores the boundaries of gender roles or outright denies their existence.

I went to this great gender bender last night, where I met this kick-ass guy—at least I thought so because of his skirt.

geotard
A person who is incapable of figuring out how to get from point A to B without instructions like "turn at the pretty blue house." A person who does not know which direction is north. A person who points in the

wrong direction when they are talking about a place. Combination of "geography" and "retard."

If I have to tell him how to get there one more time, I'm going to kick him in his geotard ass!

germaphobe

Any person who is obsessed with cleanliness and defeating bacteria. These individuals will turn on faucets with their elbows and hand-sanitize on an hourly basis.

Tiffany was such a germaphobe she wouldn't even eat a Skittle off the carpet, though it was well within the five-second rule.

get a grip

Another way of saying "take it easy" or "stop being so paranoid already!"

I told Robbie that he needs to get a grip— and I don't mean on my panty hose, either!

get big

An action in which one exceeds the normal outcome. For example: If you are about to eat more food than average, you might say, "I am going to get big in the kitchen." Can be used in reference to eating, fighting, taking a test, anything.

Somebody just got big in the bathroom.

get 'er done

A redneck term used to prod a fellow to complete a task, like finishing a beer.

Get 'er done, boy! Finish that natty!

get her jersey

To obtain a female's name and phone number.

Yeah, that drunk girl ruined my chances with her friend. You know I had to get her jersey, though!

get hot

Kick it up and step up your game, because you are becoming weak.

A cat sweatshirt and Uggs? Get hot!

get Irish

To get drunk.

Me and my friends are getting Irish at Molly's tonight.

get low

When a female's buttocks get down to the floor and they work it.

Yo, look at dat girl get low.

get more ass than a toilet seat

Implying that this "pimp" gets more action than you could ever imagine. Often used by poseurs and white people who can't rap. Perfect comeback: "You get as much ass as a urinal. Snap."

Idiot: You're gay.

Me: You've probably never even made out with anyone.

Idiot: You kidding? I get more ass than a toilet seat.

Me: Yeah, right. You get as much ass as a urinal.

Idiot: You're gay.

get retarded

The act of getting so drunk that you act like you are mentally retarded.

Tyler wanted to get retarded this weekend and accomplished his mission when he couldn't even get out of the van without falling.

get that dirt off your shoulder

Shaking them haters off; to brush off negative energy of statements made about you.

Brandon hates on me all day. Man, I gotta get all this dirt off my shoulder.

get your learn on

To study or become more educated.

Girl, you need to go to the library and get your learn on.

get your shine on

To unexpectedly exceed the expectations of one's peers in a public setting.

Get your shine on tonight, Janelle; no one knows you're an amazing dancer because you never get on the floor.

GF

1. Chatting acronym for girlfriend.

Soz, I have plans w/ the gf 2nite.

2. Gaming acronym on Jedi-Outcast: "Good Fight." Usually said after a light saber duel.

Good luck and GF.

GGG

Acronym for "good, giving, and game."

I didn't think my wife would go for that sex game but she was GGG.

ghetrosexual

A ghetrosexual is a hip-hop coolio who spends as much time preening as a metrosexual, but still fronts as if he's a badass gangster from the 'hood.

That kid ain't no gangsta, he uses Kiehl's lotion and shit. He's just a damn punk ghetrosexual.

ghettiquette

Socially acceptable behavior in the ghetto. Good manners in a bad neighborhood.

It is considered good ghettiquette to pour out the first drink of your forty to honor your dead homies. It is considered bad ghettiquette to mess up the rotation. Puff, puff, pass.

dictionary

ghetto booty

A firm, big, tight-packed ass.

Dawg, look at that girl's ghetto booty!

ghost ride

Getting out of your car while it is moving and dancing around, on top, or behind it. Ghost riding was popularized with the wave of hip-hop known as hyphy and with songs by E-40 and the Federation. Also: "ghost ride the whip."

Me and my boy were ghost riding the Tahoe last night.

gigaholic

A geek who just needs to have the latest and fastest computer.

He's such a gigaholic. There is more free space on his hard drive than in his apartment.

gilligan

A stupid, often clumsy and dimwitted individual. Makes random noises such as *"Margh!"* but is not as dumb as they seem.

Gilligan farted in assembly again, then laughed when people said he shat himself.

gimp

1. An insult implying that someone is incompetent, stupid, etc. Can also be used to imply that the person

GHOST RIDE

Ghost riding started in California and has spread all over the United States. A television station in Cleveland said ghost riding can be dangerous—not just because it's illegal, but because "ghosts are not very good drivers." In Nebraska, the *Lincoln Journal Star* reported that a teenager ghost rode a tractor—"but no hip-hop music was involved."

is uncool or can't/won't do what everyone else is doing.

Dude, quit being a gimp and take a hit!

2. A sex slave or submissive, usually male, as popularized by the movie *Pulp Fiction.*

Bring out the gimp!

ginormous

Expansive, vast, large beyond belief.

Holy shit! That is Steve's girlfriend?? She's so ginormous even the dudes at IHOP would be like, "Daaayyyyymmmm!"

girl crush

Feelings of admiration and adoration that a girl has for another girl, without wanting to shag said girl. A nonsexual attraction. Boys have boy crushes.

I have a girl crush on the girl from the band. She can sing, she's gorgeous, and she's intelligent. I want to be her.

girlfriend button

The button on the controller of an Xbox or PS2 you have to press to pause the game when your girlfriend wants to talk.

She said, "We need to talk." So I pressed the girlfriend button to pause my Madden game.

girlfriend-in-training

A female companion who is more than a friend, but not quite a full-fledged girlfriend. Often becomes a full-fledged girlfriend.

My girlfriend-in-training and I are talking about taking the next step and going out.

The analog to girl crush is "man crush," and in a segment on MSNBC in 2005, Alison Stewart explained the man crush to her viewers. She cited Urban Dictionary when trying to explain "the meaning and the mystery of the man crush," specifically in the then-developing friendship between Bill Clinton and George Bush Sr.

GIRL CRUSH

girlfriend voice

The change in pitch or tone of a man's voice when talking to his significant other. The girlfriend voice is characterized by a higher pitch and a more effeminate tone with scattered pet names and childish words. This type of speech is usually frowned upon when used in the presence of other men. When a man uses this voice he will usually receive a fair amount of ridicule.

Did you hear Bob's wicked girlfriend voice when he was talking to Lisa? Let's whoop his ass!

girly man

A man who is cowardly or pathetic; not macho.

To those critics who are so pessimistic about our economy, I say: Don't be economic girly men!

glib

Showing little thought; marked by a lack of intellectual depth. Tom Cruise accused Matt Lauer of being glib in an interview.

Tom: Matt, Matt, Matt, you're glib. You don't even know what Ritalin is. Here's the problem: You don't know the history of psychiatry. I do.

glitterati

Social elites. Famed, fashionable, adorable, and learned. The beautiful people.

Glitterati consists of fashion labor owners, celebrity socialites, actors and actresses, and other useless leeches to society.

globfrag

Word coined from "globalization" and "fragmentation"; as the world becomes more globalized with increasing technology and knowledge, more fragmentation occurs among individuals and societies.

You only need to look into a person's bedroom to realize the seriousness of globfrag. He is stuck on his computer 24/7 with instant knowledge from all over the globe at his fingertips, yet he does not know what his family is up to.

glom

To cling with sudden suction.

She glommed on to him like a duck on a june bug.

gloom rock

A rock and roll band that sounds haunting, dark, cryptic, and melancholy.

Person 1: You know of any cool "gloom rock" bands?

Person 2: Yeah! Try Interpol, She Wants Revenge, or Editors.

glory hole

A hole that has been clandestinely drilled into a stall partition in a public restroom. Used to either spy on one's neighbor in the adjacent stall, or to facilitate sexual contact.

There's a glory hole in the men's room. I love this bar!

GLOBFRAG

It's a mouthful, but "globfrag" tries to put a name to the paradoxical feeling of isolation we have even though we're more connected than ever.

ud

glove

A condom.

No love without the glove.

glove up

The act of putting on a condom before getting it on.

Guy 1: My girl will not let me anywhere near her these days unless I glove up.

Guy 2: Are you kidding? You have to glove up, man! I'm so careful, I won't even touch my girl without mittens, forget about a glove!

g money

Gangsta.

What up, g money?

gnar

A shortened version of "gnarly," meaning high on the scale of dangerousness and coolness. Often used among the skateboard crowd.

That switch heel flip was gnar.

mo'urban

go
To be tight or clean.

I like your whip. That go.

go award show
To get all tearful and emotional in front of an audience.

David went all award show in front of everyone when he found out he was getting promoted to HMFIC.

go-cup
A term used in New Orleans to refer to the plastic cups given by bars to their patrons so they might take drinks off of the premises, as in to-go drinks or at closing time.

It's closing time, guys. Want your beer in a go-cup?

go dark
To go silent. You don't speak or communicate with anyone for a given period on time. It is a way of protecting yourself from someone who would do you harm.

The clan is onto me. I'm going dark.

godbot
Someone programmed from birth to follow religious leaders' every wish; often indoctrinated in Christian fellowships closed off to free thinkers.

There were maybe forty godbots on the sidelines with signs threatening us with hell and such.

go down
Happen, occur.

Yo, bro, what's goin' down?

god shot
A shot in a game that seems very lucky, almost as if God intervened and changed the path of the ball.

Mike was surrounded by enemy players. He made a roarlike noise, waved everyone off with the ball, pretended to turn, got off balance, then shot and scored. Bob yelled, "Dude, you see that freshman score that god shot?"

Godwin's law
A term that originated in the early days of the Internet; Godwin's law states that as an online argument grows longer and more heated, it becomes increasingly likely that somebody will bring up Adolf Hitler or the Nazis. When such an event occurs, the person guilty of invoking Godwin's Law has effectively forfeited the argument.

Person 1: Dude, shut up. Nobody cares what you think.

Person 2: Oh, so now you're trying to censor me? Like the Nazis did in Germany?

Person 1: Godwin's Law—you're out!

go for a McShit
When you go into McDonald's for the sole purpose of using the

bathroom. If challenged by a spotty staff member, then your declaration that you will buy food afterward is a McShit with Lies.

Pull over, I need to go for a McShit.

go Huxtable
To settle down, find a good job, and start a family.

She is so fine, I could totally go Huxtable with that chick.

goil
Jersey speak for "girl."

Hey, she's one hot goil!

going forward
"In the future" or "somewhere down the road." In most companies, it almost seems like grounds for dismissal to issue a press release without mentioning something "going forward." Going forward, you will likely see this turning up everywhere.

Our company expects to make a profit going forward, and we don't expect any downsizing going forward.

gold
An expression used for describing a positive situation, experience, or object, or for showing appreciation.

We had a good time at the club last night. It was gold!

golden brown
Heroin.

I wish to inject some golden brown into my pulsating vein.

golden paw
The act of enticing a partner to have sex with you when they have said no. Usually involves caressing, teasing (very important), stroking, kissing, and general foreplay.

Guy 1: So did you get anywhere with Lucinda?

Guy 2: Finally. It took a serious golden paw to do it.

goldfish
Someone with an extremely short memory, or one who is extremely absentminded. Derived from the evolutionary defense mechanism of the goldfish in order to stave off insanity due to boredom: "Wow, look at that pretty plastic tree . . ." "Wow, look at that pretty plastic tree . . ." "Wow, look at that pretty plastic tree."

Damn, that Sue is such a goldfish. She just does the same dumb shit over and over again.

golf clap
Sarcastic applause, like the applause given when someone drops their food tray in a cafeteria.

He wanted us to be impressed. I showed

him just how impressed I was with the golf clap.

go make me a sandwich

A saying used when one person completely dominates another person in a game, contest, sport, etc. Implies that the winner has complete possession of the broken competitor, thus placing the loser in a condition of servitude.

We're not playing again—I just beat you fifty times in a row! I think it's time for you to go make me a sandwich.

go medieval on someone's ass

To lose one's temper on; to lose one's emotional equilibrium and act cruel or savage to somebody.

He went absolutely medieval on us!

gomer

Someone who acts stupid, makes an ass out of him or herself, has blond moments, is ignorant, naive, an idiot, and clumsy.

Dude, you are such a gomer! I can't believe you knocked that over and ruined my sofa.

gonzo

1. Crazy, madcap, unwieldy, or anarchistic.

There were people running around everywhere, it was pure gonzo!

2. A style of first-person pornography, from the view of the camera operator.

Half the adult videos you can rent fall into the gonzo genre.

good call

To make the wisest of the wise decisions to get out of a tough situation.

Good call on pulling the emergency brake to slow us down.

Goo-diligence

Using Google to mediate a dispute between two parties or to do appropriate research.

Milka: Is it a blind date?

Sunny: Sort of, but I did my Goo-diligence on him, and he's okay.

good lookin' out

A phrase used to show appreciation to someone who helped you out.

Jeremy: Yo, James, you want a soda?

James: Fo sho. Good lookin' out, dogg, I'm hella thirsty.

Googlectual

A person who calls upon obscure information they found on Google.com to appear more knowledgeable than they are. Rampant on most discussion boards.

A noted Googlectual, Tom often pasted massive articles he'd never actually read.

Google drift

To drift aimlessly between subjects of interest by finding them accidentally on a web search for something else.

Jordan: I was looking for information on the Holocaust and I found a lot of neat sites with historical facts about Germany.

Rick: Oh, so you were Google drifting.

Googlesearch fan

A person who claims to like a band, artist, author, etc., but in fact can only name works, songs, band members, etc., by searching for them on Google.com.

I was talking to Jimmy online last night about Pink Floyd. But I'm sure he doesn't actually like them. He's just a Googlesearch fan.

go ones

To have a one-on-one contest, usually on the basketball court, but sometimes fisticuffs.

If you think you're so good, let's go ones on the court and I'll school you.

go postal

To lash out violently and at random, often in a blind rage. Term taken from the incidents of workplace violence involving U.S. Postal Service workers.

After finding her computer's wallpaper had been changed to David Hasselhoff again, Jane went postal on her fellow workers.

Gore effect

The phenomenon of unseasonably cold temperatures, driving rain, hail, or snow whenever Al Gore visits an area to discuss global warming.

Al Gore visited Australia two weeks before summer began and the Gore Effect struck. According to a November 16, 2006, article in the Age: "Ski resort operators gazed at the snow in amazement. Parents took children out of school and headed for the mountains. Cricketers scurried amid bullets of hail as Melbournians traded lunchtime tales of the incredible cold."

got it going on

When a really hot girl has an excellent figure, a lot of class, and an extremely friendly demeanor.

Dude, check out Irina—she has got it going on!

go to the dentist

To drive very slowly, as if to delay one's arrival at an unpleasant destination. Also: "go to the proctologist."

That idiot up ahead must be going to the dentist.

government cheese

Money through welfare.

I get my government cheese on the first of the month.

government name

Birth or given name; not a nickname, porn star name, or secret identity.

My mom calls me Honey, but when I get her angry she yells at me by my government name.

grabasstic

Having the qualities of a playground game of grab-ass, i.e., totally chaotic and disorganized.

John's presentation at the meeting was so grabasstic that no one knew what the hell he was getting at.

grade digger

Girl who only talks to you for help with her classes.

Deron: Yo, who was that chick at the union?

Warren: Nothing. Just a grade digger.

gradumacate

To successfully complete four years of edumacation with passing grades, capped off by attending gradumacation.

When she gradumacated, Ellen whooped and hollered for joy, because she realized the joys that edumacation brings.

gramps champ

The overly slow and cautious driver, usually elderly but not necessarily, who manages to stay in front of you in traffic. They turn where you want to turn, exit where you want to exit, and go into the same parking lot you're heading for, and so they are always in the lead. You have trouble passing them because there's only one lane or traffic volume is just too busy.

Jack: How come you're so late? The movie's about to start!

Danny: I was rushing, but I got stuck behind two or three gramps champs on the way here! It was so annoying!

granny gear

1. The smallest of chainrings on a bicycle with three chainrings. So easy to pedal your grandmother could ride it.

That hill was so steep, I wish my bike had a granny gear to get up it.

2. An extremely low first gear in a four-speed truck transmission used for climbing steep hills, moving slowly over bad terrain, or driving slowly.

We drove to the top of Mount Bross (14,172 feet) in granny gear.

grape drink

The ghetto version of grape juice. The ingredients are sugar, water, and purple.

What the hell is juice? I want some grape drink, baby!

grape smuggler

When a man wears tight pants.

Check it out—Louis is a grape smuggler.

grasshopper

Someone learning from a wiser master. Often used in mockery when something is common knowledge that is easily forgotten. Similar to "padwan."

Man 1: It took me three days to download the latest version of Priston Tale.

Man 2: Three days? wtf, I downloaded it in thirty-four minutes.

Man 1: Not everyone has broadband, grasshopper.

gravy train

A job where no work is involved; to get paid for doing nothing.

Look over there—Brian is riding the gravy train again. All he does is stand around and talk when he's at work.

gray market

Marketing term for older buyers.

The gray market buys a lot of Viagra.

graze

1. To eat a lot of food without actually having a proper meal, usually in the context of picking at food that is readily available at a buffet.

OK, I'm off to the buffet to graze for a while.

2. To eat food in a grocery store, then not pay for it. Usually done while legitimately shopping at said store.

I was so hungry by the time I got to the Stop & Shop, I ended up grazing a bit—I had an apple, some Fritos, and a chocolate milk.

greenery

Marijuana.

Wanna go fetch some greenery?

green the light

A term used by a frustrated person who believes he or she can ask the help of a higher power to make a traffic light turn green for him or her. Originates from firemen who actually have the power to make the light turn green.

Green the light!

Gray-Lo

A woman too old to be dressing like J-Lo but who does it anyway. Similar to "mutton dressed as lamb."

Simmer down, Gray-Lo, and stop wearing miniskirts.

grifter

Someone who swindles you through deception or fraud. Synonyms include "fraudster," "con artist," "cheater," "confidence man," "scammer," "hustler," "swindler," etc.

That grifter swindled me out of $250,000!

grill

1. One's personal business.

Why you all up in my grill, fool?

2. One's teeth/smile.

Damn, boy, you're gonna get knocked in the grill.

3. A gold or diamond plate that is molded for your teeth. It is decorated with diamonds and/or gold. Usually worn by rappers: Nelly, Paul Wall, Mike Jones, and many others. Also: "grillz."

How much did ya grill cost?

4. To stare one down. Can be good or bad. If you grill the opposite sex it usually implies an interest in them. If heterosexuals grill the same sex, it usually means they don't like them, are testing them, and wouldn't mind smacking the shit outta them.

Good: Hey, buck, that girl is grillin' you hardcore. Go talk to her.

Bad: If that punk don't stop grillin', I'm goin' to see if he's got a problem.

grippy

A word used to describe *The Colbert Report*. Refers to the hard-hitting truthiness of news anchor Stephen Colbert.

Wow, Stephen Colbert is so grippy!

grommet

Young, annoying, rubbish skateboarder, roller blader, surfer, snowboarder, all snakeboarders, etc.

Get off the ramp, ya grommet!

grool

"Cool" and "good/great" mixed together.

Oh my God! This food is grool!

Groundhog Day

The same day over and over. Doing the same things repetitively. From the movie of the same name starring Bill Murray.

My life never changes. Every day is Groundhog Day. Eat, work, sleep.

grow a pair

To gather one's courage and do what needs to be done. Sometimes used as a call to action. Often used as an insult.

Steve backed out of our skydiving trip, so I told him to grow a pair and do it.

grow op

Suburban house that is actually a concealed indoor marijuana plantation. Grow-ops are usually loaded with high intensity lights for the crop, and often have illegally bypassed electrical meters, both to reduce costs and to prevent their detection by electrical consumption. They are often detected because of their heat—either via infrared thermography, or in colder climates, because snow melts on the roof faster than on other houses in the neighborhood. Some larger scale grow ops are installed in industrial buildings, rather than in residential areas.

You know that suspicious house down the street? The cops raided it today. It's a grow op!

grubtastic

Used to describe a particularly good food.

My god, this oatmeal is grubtastic!

GSBI

Acronym for "good-sounding bad idea." An idea that sounds exciting or plausible, but upon further thought or execution is revealed to be astoundingly dumb and/or dangerous.

Cat decided to ride her bike to school as exercise, disregarding the fact it was ten-plus miles away and she needed to be there in thirty minutes. She earned detention for her GSBI.

GU

Acronym for "geographically undesirable."

Great guy and all, but totally GU—he lives all the way in Boerum Hill!

guap

Cash money, usually referring to $1,000.

I need to work my hours. I really need to get this guap, son.

guitar face

The act of making an unusual face while playing the guitar. The look typically resembles a look of pain, intense ecstasy, or sometimes even plain old gas.

John Mayer has some crazy guitar face.

guitar sex

When two guitar players face each other, stand very close together, and rock out. This typically occurs onstage at a concert, where many voyeurs are present in the audience to observe the sexual encounter. Guitar sex often coincides with a guitargasm and frequently features guitar face by one or more of the involved parties. Guitar sex can also occur between a guitar player and a bass player, a guitar player and a keytar player, or any combo of two people playing guitarlike instruments.

Person 1: Dude, did you check out the Flecktones concert last week?

Person 2: Yeah, man, Béla Fleck and Vic Wooten were totally having guitar sex!

gunt

Bulging area found on large older women between the waist and the genital area.

My sixth-grade teacher had a gunt like a freakin' inner tube!

guppie

A gay yuppie.

Guppie: I live in a nice, big apartment, do what I want, have a great job, travel, eat out when I feel like it. No kids. High disposable income. And my mom loves my boyfriend.

gut bomb

A loaded Coney dog or chili dog. Occasionally misused to also describe one of those bite-size late-night greasy spoon hamburgers with grilled onions, which technically is known as a "slider."

After the bar closes let's stop on the way home and get a six-pack of gut bombs.

guy code

The honor and respect all guys should show to their friends. You can never talk to, hang out with, or do anything nice for my girl unless it is first approved by me. Furthermore, you cannot change your relationship with her if we ever break up.

You let her sleep over at your house last night? I don't care if nothing happened, man. You broke the guy code.

guyliner

Eyeliner for guys.

Many of today's flamboyant rock stars, but most notably Brandon Flowers of the Killers, wear guyliner.

gym rat

One who spends entirely too much time partaking in muscle building, strength training, cardiovascular exercise, or aerobic activity. Specifically, one who does so at a health club or gym. Often used derogatorily by people who do not partake in or understand this lifestyle. Some self-proclaimed gym rats use the term as a status symbol or for positive reinforcement.

I prefer to work out at home. I don't need to hang around a bunch of gym rats.

dictionary

H

hair compensation syndrome

Where someone who is going bald grows more hair out on the sides of their head to cover it up or compensates for it with distracting facial hair, e.g., very large sideburns, huge mustaches, goatees, etc.

Look at that old dude's huge burns! Classic case of hair compensation syndrome.

half-assed

Someone does a job at about 50 percent quality.

This car is fallin' apart. Those mechanics did a really half-assed job.

half a virgin

Used in the movie *Mean Girls*. You are a half virgin if you have participated in sexual acts but have not had actual sex. Also: "technical virgin."

I'm half the virgin I used to be.

half mast

Halfway to a boner.

He was turned on half-mast.

half-your-age-plus-seven

The rule to define the youngest that a romantic interest can be before the relationship is indecent.

Twenty-six-year-old Barbara waited patiently until Jack turned 20, fulfilling the half-your-age-plus-seven rule, before pursuing him romantically.

halfsies

Splitting a cost equally between two people.

Dude, do you want to go halfsies with me on that killer mud pie?

hammered

Heavily inebriated, though to a lesser extent than "shitfaced."

Man, I'm gonna go out and get hammered tonight.

hand hold-up

In celebration, when one person goes for a high five and another goes to pound it fist to fist. A slight moment of confusion occurs, normally resolved in two to twenty seconds.

When Fred and Steve went to congratulate each other for scoring with two hotties, a hand hold-up occurred.

hanger appeal

The attractiveness of a garment when viewed on a hanger (rather than being worn). A garment has hanger appeal if it looks good "on the rack" and would entice someone to look more closely, and perhaps try it on and buy it.

Girl, these tops don't have hanger appeal. They don't look good til you put them on.

hanging wedgie

When a person or a group of people grab your tighty whities and hang you on a coat hook, doorknob, etc.

When I was in the ninth grade and changing after PE in the locker rooms, some seniors grabbed me by my tighty whities and gave me a hanging wedgie.

hangry

When lack of food causes you to become angry, frustrated, or both. An amalgam of "hungry" and "angry" invented to describe that feeling you get when you are at a restaurant and have been waiting over an hour to get the meal you ordered.

Damn! Where is that steak I ordered? We've been waiting for an hour and a half here. The service here is terrible! I'm starving! I don't know about you, but I'm starting to feel really hangry!

hapa

It literally means "half" in Hawaiian. It was originally meant to describe someone who was part Hawaiian, part whatever. But the term has come to mean half Asian, half white to a lot of people.

She's hapa haole (a common term in Hawaii that means half white).

happy circuit

A brain neural circuit that makes you think that things will be better, easier, or more successful than is actually possible; a happy circuit is made of neurons and a neurotransmitter. Also: "happy circuit board."

When the voltage of his happy circuit reaches the threshold, he neglects to pay attention to imminent personal danger, regarding it as someone else's responsibility.

happy hour hottie

A girl who looks very hot after a few drinks but actually is ugly as hell.

Travis: Damn, you hooked up with a happy hour hottie last night!

Bill: Yeah, I know, I had too much to drink.

happy place

That place inside all of us where we are happy and get the warm fuzzies. Our happy places are where we are insulated from the shitheads we encounter.

I'm in my happy place and I'm not mad at the world anymore!

hard charger

A badass who floors it at a stoplight and goes peeling off down the road.

Girlfriend: Oh, my supercool boyfriend! You are such a hard charger in your Ford Ranger!

Boyfriend: Hell, yeah.

hardcore

Intense; relentless.

This girl just spent a year train-hopping around the country surviving only on Dumpster-dived food and clothing. She was pretty damn hardcore.

harples

Hard nipples.

I'm so cold, I've got harples.

hasselhoff

1. To run in slow motion.

Dude, quit hasselhoffing it and come here. Jackass!

2. To bother or harass.

The actor, though popular in Germany, was hasselhoffing the American public with his terrible music.

3. To tempt or tease.

He stripped down to his red swim trunks in an obvious attempt to hasselhoff the women on the beach.

4. To change a colleague's desktop wallpaper to display the manly physique of David Hasselhoff.

Dear god, man! I leave my workstation for a few moments to visit the big boys' room and you've hasselhoffed me!

hasta

Bye; see you later; adios.

I'm leaving now, hasta.

haterade

A figurative drink representing a modality of thought; those who consume it are themselves consumed by the negativity with which they speak.

Damn, bro, quit doming yourself on haterade.

hater blockers

A very large pair of dark sunglasses to block out the hate from any people who are jealous of you in this world.

With my hater blockers on, them crab-ass haters can see me but I can't see them.

hater tots
Like haterade, the figurative snack you consume when you're hating on someone.

Guy 1: He acts like he's the shit because he has that Mercedes SLR.

Guy 2: Man, you need to cut down on all those hater tots you've been eating.

hat hair
Greasy or sweaty hair matted to one's head after wearing a hat for a prolonged period (generally a baseball cap).

Dude, put your hat back on, you've got a serious case of hat hair.

hatriotism
Proving your patriotism by hating the people the government tells you to hate.

Well, I guess they've added a new country to the list of our enemies. I better hate them, too, if I'm going to prove my hatriotism.

have a Cheney
To have a very adverse reaction, like a heart attack.

When the bad news hit me, I nearly had a Cheney.

haze
Potent strand of weed. The fake kind is often laced with PCP.

Smoke that haze!

headphone syndrome
When someone is wearing headphones and speaks very loudly because he or she is trying to speak over the music.

Mike: Hey, man, how's it going?

Joe: I'M FINE, WHAT'S UP WITH YOU!?

Mike: Whoa, man, watch it. You're suffering from a little bit of headphone syndrome.

head shop
A store that sells smoking implements and accessories for marijuana.

I just picked up a fine bong from the head shop in West End. Shall we go burn one?

healthy
A more politically correct word commonly used to mean "fat" or "chubby." Ironically, the person in

question is generally not healthy in the classic sense, although well-fed.

Ethel: So, doc, what's the news?

Doctor: To be honest with you, your health isn't good at all. In fact, you're extremely healthy.

heck of a job

A complete and total screw-up. From President George W. Bush's infamous comment to FEMA chief Michael D. Brown while the latter was botching the federal response to Hurricane Katrina: "Brownie, you're doing a heck of a job."

Ben Affleck, you did a heck of a job on Gigli.

hecka

Word used by young children before they are old enough to use "hella" without getting in trouble.

This hecka sucks monkey butt!

hectivity

Hectic + activity = hectivity.

In an unusually busy place where people are stressed out: What's with all the hectivity?

hell to the no

A phrase used to express disbelief, shock, disgust, or incredulity.

Guy 1: Hey, man, where are we?

Guy 2: Alabama.

Guy 1: Aw hell to the no!

hemo

Homosexual emo person.

The son of the secretary of the treasury in the movie Wedding Crashers *is a hemo.*

hentai

1. Japanese for "pervert." Literally "strange desires."

All of the hentai on the bus were looking at my boobs.

2. In American usage it more often refers to Japanese porn, especially in cartoons. (The plural of "hentai" is just "hentai," not "hentais.")

Hide the hentai! Mom's coming!

hepcat

A musician who rocks at jazz.

That hepcat played an amazing solo during "A Night in Tunisia."

herm

A hermaphrodite.

I think my math teacher is a herm.

heroin chic

A style characterized by dark bags under the eyes, bed-head, over-sized clothing, and dark sunglasses. Despite looking like a bit of a slob, these individuals give off an air of confidence and glamour, a certain haughtiness amid their substance-abusing, crucifix-wearing, and generally unhealthy appearance.

Kate Moss and Johnny Depp are both heroin chic.

heteroflexible

A person who identifies themselves as primarily heterosexual but can find the same sex sexually appealing.

Most girls I know are heteroflexible.

heteromo

1. A straight man who says or does something that makes him appear gay.

Even though Brian sings show tunes and wears a lot of pink, he is not actually gay, he is just a heteromo.

2. A very straight-acting gay man. No one will ever guess that he is gay and no matter how well your gaydar works, you'll never think of him as a homosexual.

Who would have thought Eric was gay? He was such a heteromo. No wonder my gaydar missed him.

hick hop

A blend of two musical styles: country and rap. Made popular by Cowboy Troy, otherwise known as Troy Coleman.

Rap fan: I did not like country music until I heard hick hop.

Country fan: Well, I did not like rap til I heard hick hop.

high and tight

A military style haircut where the sides are cut extremely short. The hair on top is usually cut just a little longer. Sometimes the hair between the sides and top is faded, sometimes not.

When I turned blue at the end of basic training I had a high and tight.

high beams

When the nipples of a woman can be obviously seen through her clothing. The larger the protrusion the brighter the beam.

I was over at the frozen food section and I noticed a lot of high beams.

H

high maintenance

Requiring a lot of attention. When describing a person, high-maintenance usually means that the individual is emotionally needy or prone to overdramatizing a situation to gain attention.

Although he was a nice boy, his low self-esteem made him high-maintenance.

high school hero

A guy with a shitty job and no life in his twenties who dwells on how good his life was in high school.

High school hero: I loved Taft High. I scored in every football game. Then I scored with the ladies!

high-speed chicken feed

A term used by truck drivers looking for a buzz.

Anybody got any high-speed chicken feed, come in?

highway salute

An extended middle finger from a fist thrust forth while driving in a gesture of anger toward the person to which it is aimed.

That prick is tailgating me. I'm going to give him the ol' highway salute.

himbo

The male version of a bimbo, whore, or slut.

He's such a himbo that he'd sleep with anything that has, or had, a pulse.

hindspite

Looking back on a situation or event, regretting that you didn't do what you should have done, and developing malicious ill will because of it. Similar to standard regret, but someone else is gonna have to pay for it.

In hindspite, I really should have used call blocker. Now I'm gonna have to kick someone's ass.

hippinese

The dialect of hippies.

I can't understand a word Sunshine or Rainbow says, because they only speak hippinese.

hip pop

Hip-hop music that crosses over to Top-40 pop charts.

This Top-40 station plays pop, hip-hop, rock, and hip pop.

hip replacement

The process of introducing a formerly cool person to a product or idea that attempts to make them cool again. Reinventing an individual's public persona through association or action.

Quentin Tarantino gave John Travolta a hip replacement with Pulp Fiction.

hit a lick

To gain a shitload of money in a short amount of time

Aw, dawg, I hit a lick this week at the casino.

hit it

To have sex.

Guy: You look hot.

Girl: Thanks.

Guy: Can I hit it?

McDonald's used "I'd hit it" as a catch phrase in an advertising campaign in 2005. The advertisements showed the words, "Double Cheeseburger? I'd hit it." The definitions given on urbandictionary.com use "I'd hit it" as an expression of a desire to have sexual relations; is that what McDonald's meant? For future campaigns, we recommend their copywriters keep Urban Dictionary handy.

I'D HIT THAT

hit me on the hip

Calling someone on their cell phone, pager, or two-way.

Most chicks have to call me at home, but I let her hit me on the hip.

hizzle

House.

Fo shizzle, get up out dis hizzle.

HMFIC

Acronym for "head mothafucka in charge." The boss; someone to be reckoned with. Used to denote, usually in jest, that a person is in charge of a situation.

The coach is the HMFIC. What he says, goes.

hoasis

Lots of hos in one spot, no dudes.

It's like a hoasis up in this bitch.

hobeau

An unclean boyfriend.

He is such a hobeau, with his long hair and beard. He hasn't showered since they invented water but I luv him anyway.

hobosexual

The opposite of metrosexual; one who cares little for one's own appearance.

The first documented hobosexual was John the Baptist.

ho ho ho

Santa's cry, or three prostitutes.

Ho ho ho, it's Christmas!

ho hound

To be all over girls who you like, not giving them any room to breathe.

Guy 1: Yo, where's James?

Guy 2: He doesn't have time for us now. He's busy ho hounding, constantly up that girl's ass.

hold it down

To take care of oneself and/or one's surroundings in another's absence.

What's up, America? G.W. holdin' it down in the big D.C. ya heard.

holla back girl

A girl willing to be treated like a doormat or booty call. She will allow guys to do whatever they want with her and will just wait for them to "holla back" at them.

Jermaine fools around with Aisha. Thinking he likes her, she waits around for him to make contact with her again. Aisha is a holla back girl.

Hollywood

A sarcastic nickname for someone who is unreasonably vain. Especially effective when used on a man who constantly checks his reflection.

Looking good, Hollywood.

Hollywood hang up

When you suddenly hang up the phone. Typical people will give some

indication the conversation is over: "See you later," "Good-bye," "Talk to you soon," etc. But as Hollywood movies have taught us, this is not necessary. When you are finished with what you have to say, hang up.

Tom: Did you get the memo I sent you, Rob?

Rob: Yes, but I will read it later. (Click.)

homefry

Buddy, homedog, best friend.

What's crackalackin', my homefry?

homie

Shortened version of homeboy; your close friend.

Whassup, homie?

homoblivious

Not having the ability to recognize homosexuals as homosexuals; a lack of gaydar.

He was so homoblivious that he didn't know that guy was coming on to him.

homorobotic

Being of homosexual, and robotlike nature.

C-3PO was really homorobotic.

hooch

1. Alcohol.

Pass me the hooch. I'm quite depressed.

2. Marijuana.

Oh my God, that hooch last night was great!

3. A whore.

What a hooch!

hood rat

A girl who sleeps with various men in the neighborhood. Usually noticeable via her slacking standards of personal care.

Sissy is a hood rat!

hood rich

You managed to finance the Escalade despite your terrible credit, but you don't have any money for gas. You live in your mom's house but wear blingin' chains. Translation: Someone in the ghetto who spends money they obviously don't have; a repo-man's wet dream.

Girl drives a Lexus and got a fifty-four-inch flat-screen TV. She is hood rich.

hood vision

When you can't fathom the idea of a world existing outside of your neighborhood. A small-town mentality in the middle of a city.

People in Williamsburg have hood vision. They think the L is the only train line in Brooklyn.

hoof it

To travel by foot; to walk.

His car broke down, so he had to hoof it into town.

hooker casual

Just as there is business attire for formal business situations and business casual for social situations that have potential implications for business, so, too, is there "hooker-casual" dresswear for those times when you kind of look like a ho who's presently off-duty.

You probably shouldn't dress hooker casual to class today.

hop-along

Wannabe; someone who rides someone else's coattails; unwanted sidekick.

Dammit, does that hop-along little brother of yours have to come with us on every trip out of the house?

hope couture

The item of clothing you keep for years hoping in vain you might fit back into it someday.

This pair of jeans is kinda hope couture for me.

hork

To steal something, though not usually applicable to shoplifting or grand theft.

I turned around for five minutes and someone horked my Pepsi from the fridge at work.

hornophobia

A psychological condition that causes paranoia around people with increased sexual desire.

Leila freaked out when that couple started making out. She appears to be suffering from hornophobia.

horse

Heroin.

Keith Richards did so much horse in his lifetime that his blood type is China white.

hoser

A clumsy, stupid person who drinks beer excessively. Commonly used in Canada.

You hoser, eh!

hoss

A southern colloquial nickname for partner; a term of friendship.

You betta' get that grass mowed, hoss.

hostage lunch

Meal purchased by the company, often pizza, and delivered for employees whose bosses require them to attend a meeting or work over their lunch hour.

I was planning on running some errands over my lunch hour, but the VP is keeping us in a meeting. At least he ordered us hostage lunch.

hot coffee

A "hidden" secret in the Rockstar game Grand Theft Auto: San Andreas that allows players to play sex mini-games. This fiasco has resulted in the game being rated AO (Adults Only) and pulled from the shelves of most game stores.

I finally got to hot coffee in GTA, but I got bored of it after a few minutes and returned to my favorite source for free adult content: the Internet.

hot mess

Someone who is dressed poorly or whose hair is not done; a person who is poor in appearance.

She looks like a hot mess.

hot monkey sex

Wild, unabashed sexual activity that leaves one or more of the participants howling like a deranged monkey.

After five hours of athletic and dexterous hot monkey sex, both Sarah and Gene were ready for a good night's sleep.

hot snack

The small amount of acidy puke you have to swallow when you are just sitting around minding your own business and you have a little unexpected burp.

Dude, I was just talkin' to my girl and out of nowhere I had to swallow a hot snack without her noticing.

hott

Sexually attractive. Also: "hot."

Damn! He's hott!

house elf

Someone who does everything his parents tell him to do, even bogus things like ironing a bunch of clothes, vacuuming a car he doesn't drive, fixing vegetables, etc. Some house elves have cell phones that go off at random times, always from the parent asking him to do a task, and because of his house elf–nature he is forced to obey. Taken from the Harry Potter series, in which a house elf named Dobby had to do whatever his master asked of him and could only become free if his master presented him with clothes.

Why does Johnny always iron the clothes, vacuum, and fix the vegetables when he could just refuse? He's such a house elf!

huggles

A hug and cuddle combined into one move.

I was with my girlfriend last night and I gave her lots of huggles.

huggy bear

Everything is cool, works fine, is in place.

Question: How's the new project doing?

Reply: Huggy bear.

hug it out

To hug in order to help get over anger or sadness.

Brian: Damn, I can't believe she broke up with me.

Mary: Wanna hug it out?

hump day

The middle of a workweek (Wednesday); used in the context of climbing a proverbial hill to get through a tough week.

After hump day, the weekend gets closer.

humpty

To do something in the public eye that causes irreparable damage to one's reputation and brings intense ridicule and overwhelming embarrassment. Telltale signs that one has committed a humpty and knows it (or has been informed by PR) include: appearing on every daytime and late-night talk show with nothing to promote except not being hated by the public, having your name become a verb, finding that the overwhelming hatred and ridicule for you is so strong that you become the common enemy that unites two or more groups with previously irreconcilable differences.

Did you see Tom Cruise on The Oprah Winfrey Show? *Wow, he really pulled a humpty when he jumped on the couch like an idiot.*

hurt locker

A figurative place where someone is said to be or will be, if they are getting or expect to get hurt or beaten.

With that team, you are entering a rather large hurt locker.

hXc

Abbreviation of hardcore, often related to music from the hardcore genre. Also used to describe actions or styles.

This bandana will make me look so hXc.

hydro

Hydroponically grown marijuana.

Yo, let's go blaze some hydro.

hypertasking

The simultaneous execution of an exceedingly large number of tasks. An otherwise unmanageable number of tasks that can be accomplished with an extreme level of concentration, i.e., taking multitasking to the nth degree. If going to school full-time requires multitasking, then going to school full-time, working full-time, and taking care of the family damn sure requires hypertasking.

Look at him go! That mofo is hypertasking like a Cray Supercomputer.

hyphy

Hyperactive. NorCal crunk; hyphy is to northern California as crunk is to the South. Hyphy is bringing crunk to a whole new level, just goin' all out nasty. Sometimes spelled "hyphe" or "hyphee."

Ayo, DJ, put that new E-40 single on. It's guaranteed to get the crowd hyphy.

hyphy train

A wild, mobile party with a long line of cars with all the doors open, in which occupants ghost-ride, dance on the hood and roof, and otherwise get hyphy.

The line of cars gas brake dippin' and ghost ridin' makes a hyphy train.

I call bullshit

An expression of distaste or aggravation used to call someone out on a complete falsehood. A way to say that something is at odds with a generally accepted truth.

Richard: George W. Bush is a great president.

Al: I call bullshit!

icescapee

The ice cube that ends up on the floor when you break a new tray of ice.

Person 1: What about the icescapee?

Person 2: Oh, don't worry—the dog will get it!

ickle

Another word for "little." Often used in England.

There's an ickle kitten on the doorstep.

IDGI

Acronym for "I don't get it." Used when you're confused or don't understand something.

h4x0r: 1 h4xx0or3d j00 n00b!

nub: IDGI . . .

if only

A retort that means, "What you've just said is plainly not true, although I certainly wish it were."

My ex: I'm never going to call or email you again.

Me: If only!

i-haircut

A small change in one's online identity comparable to getting a haircut, shaving, or some other real-life change in appearance.

FushDabi got an i-haircut when he changed the font he sent messages in.

I heart you

I "love" you. But not quite, usually said to someone you like, but not quite want to have sex with.

Boy: I'm sad.

Girl: No, don't be! ^.^ I heart you.

I like your style

A phrase used to express one person's endorsement of another's general style. Is also commonly used to show happiness at a person's actions. Extra emphasis is placed on the phrase when it is accompanied by a friendly point and wink at the recipient. The correct response is, "I like your moves."

Man 1: Can you lift that box? It's too heavy for me.

Man 2: Certainly.

Man 1: I like your style.

I love you like tenth-grade science class

An expression of much love and chemistry.

Guy: I love you, do you love me?

Girl: Well, I love you like tenth-grade science class.

Guy: Huh, why tenth-grade science class?

Girl: There's so much chemistry.

Guy: Oh, got it. Well, I love you like eleventh-grade science class.

Girl: Physics?

Guy: Yeah, there's so much potential.

(Guy and Girl make out like ninth-grade science class, Biology: Life or Creating It.)

imaginertia

A disinclination to think imaginatively. A block to one's imagination and originality caused by lack of inspiration; an inert imagination.

After several days of doing nothing and getting nowhere, the inventor realized he was suffering from imaginertia.

I'm bored

What you say when you have absolutely nothing to do and can find no pot. The state at which you want a meteor to fall through your ceiling and hit you in the leg, just so you'd have something to do.

Places people are bored:

1. School

2. Work

3. Sitting on a bench

4. Waiting for someone or something

5. Watching movies from before 1960

Things people do when they're bored:

1. Add words to urbandictionary.com

2. Bubble in all the a's, b's, d's, e's,

g's, o's, p's, and all the other letters with loops in them in a novel

3. Teach themselves useless skills like balancing a pencil on their nose or throwing cards

4. Try to move things with their mind

5. Watch a TV channel that only has static on it

Josh: Dude, I'm bored.

Kevin: Deal with it, you douche.

I'm just sayin'

A phrase that is used when someone is offended by something you said. This phrase then removes all the offensiveness of the previous statement, making it all good.

Ryan: That chick has nice tits!

Rob: Damn, that's my sister!

Ryan: I'm just sayin'.

Rob: Oh, okay, it's cool.

I'm-not-gay seat

The empty seat in a movie theater that two males leave between them to show the rest of the audience that they are straight.

Bob: I went to a movie with John the other day, but we left the I'm-not-gay seat, so no one thought it was weird.

infinity plus shipping and handling

Similar to "infinity plus one." It

stems from the idea that everything has shipping and handling tacked on when ordered.

Teacher: Does anybody know what's larger than infinity?

Student: Nothing.

Teacher: No, infinity plus shipping and handling.

Internet anytime minutes

What office workers use when they are being the "most productive" at their jobs.

T-roy looked at the clock and said, "Well, boys, I have two hours left to do absolutely nothing! The web don't surf itself! It's time to use up some of my Internet anytime minutes to look busy!"

Internet crack

Addictive, time-consuming web sites that have little or no benefit for abusers except to make them feel good.

MySpace, TagWorld, and porn sites are examples of Internet crack.

Internet hobo

Someone who is using their neighbor's wireless Internet connection.

My friend just bought a new high-power wi-fi card so he can connect to the neighbor's network and is now an official Internet hobo.

interrorgate

To question needlessly under the pretext of defending against terror.

The gate agent was concerned that I was only carrying with me a small carry-on bag. She summoned airport security, who proceeded to interrorgate me with a series of personal questions.

in the wind

Always on the move.

Your folks are never at home. They stay in the wind.

intoxicourse

Having sexual intercourse while piss-drunk.

Holy shit! I can't remember anything! Did I have intoxicourse last night?

intrasexual

A person who has sexual intercourse only with him or herself. They do not mate with members of either sex; rather they keep to themselves, pleasing only themselves. They are their own sex toy.

Tonette does not like men or women because she is an intrasexual and cannot be pleased by either gender.

I pity the fool

In Mr. T-glish, a comment equivalent to the English "I'd best not find out who it was."

I pity the fool who scratched my car.

iPod spamming

The act of downloading more songs than one is actually planning to listen to. This is usually done by people wishing to raise the number of songs on their iPod in an attempt to seem cooler than they actually are.

Person 1: Wow, how did Gerry get so many songs on his iPod?

Person 2: Well, I suggested a good song to him and he went and downloaded every song that band has ever made.

Iraqnophobia

An unusually strong fear of Iraq, especially its ability to manufacture and use biological, chemical, and nuclear weapons.

Now that September is here, President Bush can launch his initial public offering of stock in his newest product, Iraqnophobia.

Irish-American

What everybody in America becomes once a year on March 17.

Yea, it's St. Patrick's Day! Kiss me, I'm Irish-American (today).

Irish flu

A particularly unpleasant hangover.

Last night was great, but I have the worst case of the Irish flu today.

it is what it is

A phrase that seems to simply state the obvious but actually implies helplessness. It actually means "it will be what it is," as in "it ain't gonna change, so deal with it or don't." Has become a cliché, popular within the circles of coaches, business execs, and those of us who just want to say "It's happened. I'm going to forget about it. I'm going to move on. There is nothing that can be done about it." Also: "tough shit," "oh well," "cry me a river," and "tfb."

Driver: I can't believe the price of gas!

Attendant: It is what it is.

I was all

Expression commonly used in place of "and I said" when reenacting a past conversation. Usually followed with the response to said conversational dialogue in the form of "and (s)he was all."

"Well, I was all, 'Omigawd, he is SO buff!'" Candi explained to her friend, Maria. "And she was all, 'You're totally right about that, fa shizzle.'"

J

jack

Absolutely nothing; a shortened form of "jack shit" or "jack squat" and a synonym of "diddly."

You: Hi, honey . . . my, you're home late. What did you do today?

Your wife: Jack.

jackhole

Portmanteau of "jackass" and "asshole." Used by radio personalities Kevin and Bean (from KROQ-FM in Los Angeles) as a way of calling somebody a nasty name without actually breaking FCC edicts against foul language.

Darl McBride is a jackhole for trying to sue the Linux community for something he doesn't own.

January joiner

Someone who joins the gym in January as part of a New Year's resolution and by February is back to being a couch potato.

I can't get a treadmill until February because the January joiners are all using them.

jawesome

Awesome; used by the *Street Sharks* action figures and cartoon show.

I did jawesome on that test.

Jedi mind trick

The mind trick is something used by Jedis to persuade people to do things as they wish them to. This is generally achieved by the Jedi waving his hand slowly in front of his face and speaking slowly and clearly what they would like the person to believe. Often used in jest for when you are trying to persuade someone of something and it isn't working very well.

Bouncer: Do you have any identification?

Jedi: (waving hand) We do not need any identification.

Bouncer: You do not need any identification.

Jesus juice
Wine served in a Diet Coke can, with the purpose of getting a thirteen-year-old drunk enough to be seduced by a pale freak with a funny nose.

Shut up and drink your Jesus juice.

jiggy
1. Being down with something

Yeah, I'm jiggy wit that.

2. Having sex or messing around

I got jiggy wit your mom.

3. Exclamation meaning "sweet!" or "tight!"

Gator boots with the pimped-out Gucci suit. Jiggy!

job
Means by which at least 30 percent of your life is stolen from you to enrich the owners of a company by making useless shit that some other poor idiot in a job will buy.

My job allows me to pay endless bills and envy my friends' free time.

job job
A real job with health insurance; as opposed to an internship or the wonderful world of retail.

I'm an editor—primarily of technical documentation for my job job, but I also dabble in things like web site authoring on the side.

jones
Desire for something that may be sought irrespective of the consequences. Can apply to humans, love, drugs, whatever.

Man, I've been jonesin' for days!

joygasm
A huge feeling of pleasure, but not from sexual experiences. These feelings can come from any event or thing that makes a person feel joy.

Green Day's new video made me have a joygasm!

juju

Luck. More commonly used in the term "bad juju," or bad luck.

That is bad juju, man. Be careful.

jukebox sabotage

Implanting one's own music into another person's mind by singing or whistling a tune around that person. If successful, that person will then begin whistling or singing your song minutes later.

I whistled "Mary Had a Little Lamb" around my friend Matt one afternoon and then five minutes later I heard him whistling it down the hall. That is a textbook jukebox sabotage maneuver.

jump off

Anything that is considered good, or beneficial, to the subject; hip, chic, or in fashion.

Andrea: You goin' to the new club?

Tony: Hell, yeah—that's the jump off right there, nah mean?

jump the couch

A defining moment when you know someone has gone off the deep end. Inspired by Tom Cruise's behavior on *Oprah*.

My new boyfriend, Benny, seemed totally normal until he jumped the couch and started rubbing spicy brown mustard on his body at my family reunion.

jump the shark

When something that was once great reaches a point where it starts declining in quality and popularity. Comes from a *Happy Days* episode in which the Fonz jumped a shark on water skis.

The Brady Bunch jumped the shark the day Cousin Oliver joined the cast.

junk in the trunk

Describes a woman with a fair to good amount of ass. Generally carries a positive connotation.

I can't stand those anorexic girls. I need a girl with some junk in the trunk!

JUMP THE COUCH

Tom Cruise made "jump the couch" famous during his *Oprah* appearance in May 2005 when he declared his love for Katie Holmes. "Jump the couch" was named Slang of the Year by the Historical Dictionary of American Slang. See also "glib," "scientomogy," and "TomKitten" on urbandictionary.com.

ud

mo'urban

K

ka-ching
The sweet sound of cash. Usually associated with making (or spending) a windfall.

I'm playing the ponies with my Social Security check. Ka-ching!

keep it 100
To keep yourself real and true; to be honest and stick to the way you are, no matter what anyone else thinks.

I gotta stay focused and keep it 100 these last few weeks of high school so I can get into college. And that's real talk!

keep it gangsta
Something you say to someone when you're parting ways to remind that person to keep being a thug and not turn bitch.

Nick: Well, I'll see you later, Grandma. Thank you for that delicious Thanksgiving dinner.

Grandma: Catch ya later, my nigga. Keep it gangsta, dogg.

keep it neat
To look calm, collected, chilled out, and very confident.

Bro, I know you're whylin out right now, but those girls over there are feelin' us, so keep it neat.

keep it posi
Short for "keep it positive."

Bob: Look, I colored a picture of a lion.

Karen: It looks like shit. The color is all over the place. You didn't stay within the lines.

Mom: Hey, you two! Keep it posi, or no macaroni for lunch!

dictionary

keep steppin'

To move on from something bad.

Yo, homie, don't worry 'bout her—keep steppin'.

Kentucky doorbell

To drive up to someone's house or apartment and proceed to honk the horn until they come out, rather than going to all the trouble of exiting the vehicle and going to the door.

The neighbor across the street had a friend who would ring the Kentucky doorbell each morning at 5:00 a.m. I say "had" because me and my tire iron had a little chat with him.

kicker dog

Any dog roughly the size of a football, such as a Chihuahua or Yorkshire terrier.

I went to her house and she had three squirrelly kicker dogs running around in the living room.

kick the shoe home

To close down the pub and stumble home exhausted and inebriated.

See ya, Rory. We'll be kicking the shoe home tonight.

killjoy

Someone who wants to ruin someone else's fun.

The killjoy tattled to the apartment manager after he saw Mike enter his apartment with a gorgeous woman at midnight.

kite

Correspondence received while incarcerated.

My cuz sent me a kite . . . told me to hold it down while I'm doin' my bid.

kleptocracy

A system of government character-ized by rampant corruption and misallocation of public funds.

That country is a kleptocracy in which nothing is accomplished without greasing the palms of government officials.

Kodak courage

An extra dose of courage and the tendency to go beyond one's usual physical limits when being filmed or photographed, as in action sports such as skateboarding, snowboard-ing, and extreme skiing.

I was a bit nervous being the first to hit the jump, but when you're with the film crew you get that Kodak courage.

k-rad

One thousand times rad, just as a Kbyte or kilobyte refers to 1,000 bytes. Made popular in the 1980s in computer hacker circles. The word "rad" refers to a radical act performed by a hacker that deserves congratulations. The term originated around the same time people started talking in numbers, l1k3 th15. This type of language first started appearing on BBSes and FTP sites.

I h4v3 +h3 m05+ 733+, k-r4d 5k1llz 0n th3 n3+!!!!!!!!!!!!!!

(I have the most leet, k-rad skillz on the net!)

Kraft singles

Dollar bills. Derived from another slang term that refers to money as "cheese."

Yo, I just cashed my check, so I got a wallet full of Kraft singles. Drinks are on me!

krew

A group (usually teenagers) who have formed a small gang. Mostly consists of taggers who mark their territory with markers. Mostly nonviolent but will protect their territory.

That krew tagged up the school the other day.

krieg

Used in the heavy metal community to describe something of high quality. Originally the German word meaning "war," it was popularized as a metal term by Nargaroth's album *Black Metal Ist Krieg*.

Dude, you have to hear the new Alghazanth. It's krieg as hell.

dictionary

L

l8r

Chat expression for "later" in 1337 language.

I gotta go . . . see ya l8r.

lactard

A lactose-intolerant person.

Jasminda: Babu, do you want to get some ice cream?

Babu: Sorry, Jasminda, I can't eat ice cream—I'm a lactard.

lady lumps

Sexually appealing breasts on a woman.

Hey, check out her lovely lady lumps.

lal

Chat speak for "lacht aus laut," which is German for "laughing out loud."

Person 1: u r suxxx roflll

Person 2: lal stfu

land clam

A mass of phlegm expelled from the esophagus onto a surface such as asphalt or concrete. It is the only nonshelled mollusk known to man.

While hacking outside Lincoln Center, Charles fathered a land clam on 65th Street.

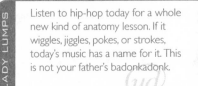

LADY LUMPS

Listen to hip-hop today for a whole new kind of anatomy lesson. If it wiggles, jiggles, pokes, or strokes, today's music has a name for it. This is not your father's badonkadonk.

mo'urban

lap dog

A person who is a subservient brown-noser to an organizational superior; someone who obediently follows authority figures without regard for their own interests or principles.

The boss likes Joe, but he's such a lap dog.

lappy

Short for laptop computer, especially old and outdated models.

What's your lappy weigh, like forty-two pounds?

lateral beauty

Someone who looks attractive from the side but not from the front.

Person 1: Damn, did you see that guy? He is hot!

Person 2: Wait till you see him head-on.

Person 1: Yikes! Now that is some lateral beauty.

later days

See you later, see you tomorrow, see you soon, see you never, see you in a bit. The main character says it at the end of every episode of *The Weekenders*, a cartoon show.

Dude A: OK, bro, I'll see you when you get back.

Dude B: Gotcha man, later days.

laugh whore

A person who laughs at all of your jokes just to gain acceptance from you. You don't mind it because it makes you feel better about yourself. Usually has a mildly obnoxious laugh to go along with his or her hair-trigger laugh reflex.

Jason: Yeah, so then I said, "Because the frog was stapled to the chicken!"

Laugh whore: Ha ha ha ha ha ha!

Jason: Yeah, I made that one up myself!

launch

To reach the point of no return in a night of drinking; you are bound to either black out, make an ass of yourself, fight, or all of the above.

Eric had launched somewhere between his sixth and seventh tequila shot. After that it was all downhill.

lawn job

Messing up someone's front lawn with your car.

I gave that stupid bitch teacher a lawn job for failing me.

lawyer ball

The art of playing the rules instead of playing a game. For example, trying to work out a walk in slow-pitch softball. Also applicable to weenies who demand free throws after the slightest contact in a pick-up basketball game and douche bags who take yardage penalties in back-yard football games.

Pops: Hit it out of the park, boy!

Son: Don't pressure me, I'm trying to work the count.

Pops: Don't play lawyer ball, son.

L bomb

When someone unexpectedly tells you that they love you. Usually comes out of the blue when you least expect it and are not prepared to respond.

Guy 1: Dude! Shannon totally dropped the L bomb on me last night!

Guy 2: Damn. What did you do?

Guy 1: I said "I love you, too."

learn you a lesson

To show someone that they are wrong or incompetent, either by punishing or humiliating them.

You think you're good at video games? Give me that controller and I'll learn you a lesson!

leetspeak

A language in which some letters are replaced with symbols or numbers, often accompanied by random and/or deliberate misspellings.

English: Peter waters the lawn.

Leetspeak: P4t4r \/\/4+3r5 t3h l3\/\/n!!

left-handed web site

A porn web site.

Ever since I lost my job job, I've been designing left-handed web sites. Eventually, I hope to make a contribution in a less . . . uhh . . . behind-the-scenes way.

legalese

The dialect the legal profession uses to hoodwink people into paying them a week's wage for an hour's work.

Attorneys use legalese to tell lies about regular people without the regular people being able to understand what's said about them.

lesbi-friends

Two women who are such close friends they seem like they are lesbians. A play on "let's be friends." Also spelled "les-bi-friends" or "lesbefriends."

When I saw those two chicks hugging, I said to myself "lesbi-friends."

less than three

The literal form of <3, which in turn is supposed to represent a sideways heart (love).

Blog comment: I less than three you, dude!

Let me get you a straw

A shortened version of the sentiment "Let me get you a straw so you can *suck it up.*" Generally more comical (read: obnoxious) than simply telling a whiner to deal.

A minor chainsaw incident occurs.

Bob: Um, could you call 911 for me?

Frank: Do it yourself.

Bob: I don't have hands anymore.

Frank: Well, let me get you a straw.

lick

Easy money, whether you jack it, hustle it, or barter for it.

I can't pay you right now. Let me just hit a lick and I'll get you your money.

lickle

To tickle by licking.

Samantha started to lickle Mandy and made her laugh.

lie to kick it

When someone tells lies or stories to fit in with the crowd.

Me: I just bought a new car!

Greg: I know, I bought a new car and a house.

Me: Come on, Greg, you don't have to lie to kick it.

lifehack

A tool or technique that makes some aspect of one's life easier or more efficient.

Web sites now exist where lifehackers can trade lifehacks—suggestions on how to reduce chaos and make their lives more enjoyable.

limousine liberal

Wealthy person who adopts the cause of the downtrodden; carries a connotation of hypocrisy. Also: "bobo," "bicoastal," or "parlor pink."

The limousine liberals oppose vouchers but send their kids to private school.

Lincolnish

Possessing the qualities of truthiness, justice, and the red-state American way. Commonly used by neocon faux journalist Stephen Colbert to describe himself.

Stephen Colbert is Lincolnish.

L

lip service

To say something but not actually do it; to pretend that you believe a certain thing but not practice that belief.

The company pays lip service to equal rights but has only one woman working for them, and she's underpaid.

lipstick lesbian

Feminine lesbian who is attracted to other feminine lesbians. They generally enjoy fashion, flowers, perfume, *Sex and the City,* lingerie, lipstick, of course, and (gasp!) passionate sex with other women.

If I wanted to date someone who looked like a man, I'd find a man. Where are all the lipstick lesbians?

livin' the dream

A good response to "How are you?" If you're really livin' the dream, hold your right hand up in a "rock!" symbol (same as sign language for "I love you"). If you are hyper-livin', hold up both hands. Can be shortened to "livin' it."

Q: Baby Helen, what's up?

A: (both hands up in "rock!" formation) Livin' it!

lockblock

When one person prematurely tries to open the passenger door on a vehicle while the driver simultaneously tries to unlock the door, causing it to relock and keep the passenger outside.

Guy 1: Hey, man, get in the car already. It's cold out there!

Guy 2: I've been trying to, but you've lockblocked me like five times in a row now!

lock it up

To keep a secret.

Dude, remember that Mary girl? I got with her last night. But hey . . . lock it up.

lot lizard

A trucker's term for a prostitute who works truck stops.

That TA is loaded with lot lizards.

loved up

High on Ecstasy.

Was that DJ really good or did I just think so because I was all loved up?

lowjack

To take something by smooth talking or strong convincing. Not as violent or non-participatory as being hijacked, being lowjacked involves one's own insecure or gullible nature.

He lowjacked me out of my bling by flattery and making me feel uncomfortable that he didn't have any!

low low

A lowrider. A car or truck with an altered suspension, such that the car rides low to the ground. May include hydraulics and specialized wheels.

We're hitting the corners in those low lows, girl.

lucktard

One who has a natural dumb luck that bails them out of any situation, regardless of severity.

Her pregnancy test was negative. Again. That lucktard.

M

Macaca

A racial slur meaning "monkey" used by Senator George Allen while campaigning in Virginia.

While campaigning, Senator George Allen made the following remark about one of his constituents—an Indian American UVA student who was born and raised in Virginia, who was filming the event: "This fellow here over here with the yellow shirt, Macaca, or whatever his name is. He's with my opponent. . . . Let's give a welcome to Macaca, here. Welcome to America and the real world of Virginia."

MacGyver

To use everyday objects you have on hand to accomplish an otherwise impossible task. From the 1980s TV series *MacGyver*, starring Richard Dean Anderson.

So I took my shoelaces, tied them together, lassoed the gas pedal with a paperclip, slid a wrench down it to change the direction of force, threaded it through the steering wheel, and attached it to the door handle, so that when I opened the car door and jumped out, the force from opening the door would cause the car to let on the gas and drive toward the men with the bazookas, letting me escape. I guess you could say I MacGyvered it.

mack

To hit on, flirt with, or seduce a female using verbal or physical means of persuasion.

I caught David macking on my wife.

madam's apple

A play on "Adam's apple," referring to the large bulge on the trachea of a woman. May be the sign of a male-to-female transvestite or transsexual, or may simply be genetics.

Holy crap! Look at that madam's apple on Ann Coulter!

madawk

A contraction of mad awkward. Can be used as an interjection in situations that are very awkward.

Guy 1: Mom walked in on me right before I was about to get laid.

Guy 2: Madawk.

mad props

A way to say "thank you."

Mad props to Christopher for that burger he made—that was really nice.

make it rain

In strip clubs, to throw money up in the air at the strippers so that it seems to be raining money onto them.

After Leroy finished trapping for the night, he went to the strip club and got ten stacks so he could make it rain the whole night.

mammograph

A celebrity signature written on a female breast, usually with a permanent marker.

Julie got a mammograph from DJ Tom on her left boob last night.

man bag

A bag with one strap worn by

metrosexual or homosexual males. Especially prevalent in cities and on college campuses.

Jack's man bag was more stylish than a backpack.

man blanket

A woman who constantly drapes herself over a man.

Lisa is such a man blanket after a few drinks.

man card

Requirement to be accepted as a respectable member of the male community. Can and should be revoked by other respectable males for doing non-respectable-male things.

We had to take away Henry's man card because he cried in public when Kristina dumped him.

mancation

When normal males engage in "guy" activities that involve sports, camping, gambling, chasing women, and most of all, drinking, among their male friends. No wives, mistresses, or girlfriends allowed. Done in order to get in touch with their male-primal roots.

Jack and I hiked twenty-five miles to trout-fish in the Sierras. With many beers and stories, it made for the perfect mancation.

man hands

Phrase to describe a woman's hands when they are "less than feminine." From the TV show *Seinfeld*.

She's got man hands!

manorexic

A male anorexic or an emaciated man.

Did you see that pathetic emo kid? He was such the manorexic.

manpanion

1. A male companion; a term used to categorize a male friend with an ambiguous characterization of sexual orientation.

Tom has never been married. He loves to spend time with Dick more than anyone. They are great manpanions.

2. A nonmonogamous homosexual companion.

He's not looking for commitment. Instead, he has several manpanions.

To better understand the manca-tion, the *Los Angeles Times* cited Urban Dictionary's definition in 2007—and added that "throwing power tools" might be a popular masculine activity to add to your itinerary. The *New York Times* said that Vince Vaughn popularized the term in the 2006 movie *The Break-Up*. One service cited by the *New York Times* sells a three-night Vegas mancation for four for $55,000.

MANCATION

man stand

When a man stands outside a shop while his wife/girlfriend/partner shops. Man standing involves looking into space or at other women, or, at multistory shopping centers, leaning on the railings of an upper floor watching the people below.

I've been doing the man stand outside New Look for an hour!

mantastic

Feeling fantastic after the successful completion of a particularly macho feat.

Following his fifth keg of beer, Kevin ripped the horn off of his pet narwhal and then nailed his porn-star girlfriend for hours. Subsequently, he felt mantastic.

David Letterman is a fan of "mantastic"; it appeared on his Top Ten Effects of Y2K list, on New Year's Eve 1999. His list said one of the effects would be that "Ricky Martin would become even more mantastic."

MANTASTIC

manterage

The guys that hang around a beautiful girl; a girl's male entourage.

Julie never goes out on a Friday night without her manterage. They just can't get enough of her.

man whore

A male who typically juggles "commitments" with multiple females at once, while engaging in noncommittal sexual relations on the side.

Although each secretly strives to be a man whore, most men spend their time looking for just one woman to sleep with.

marble ceiling

Discriminatory barrier keeping a certain class of people out of an upper echelon of American government. Distinguished from a glass ceiling because not only is this class prevented from rising to the next level, they cannot even see what is going on up there. Used by U.S. Speaker of the House Nancy Pelosi.

When my colleagues elect me as speaker on January 4, we will not just break through a glass ceiling, we will break through a marble ceiling. —Nancy Pelosi, January 3, 2007

March sadness

As opposed to March Madness, the deep, depressing feeling that comes when your brackets are completely messed up and your favorite team has lost.

Guy 1: Dude, what's wrong with Brad?

Guy 2: Ohio State lost last night—he's got a case of March sadness.

marker bee

A higher-level university student employed by a professor to mark papers. Also known as a "teacher's aide," or "T.A."

Professor Bombshell's overzealous marker bees couldn't actually find anything wrong with my paper, so they made shit up. I asked Bombshell to look it over himself and he agreed I should get a higher grade on it.

marriage

1. A license to have sex.

Conservatives are big on protecting the sacred bond of marriage.

2. What straight couples have legally and commonly don't want, and what gay couples don't have legally and commonly want.

Britney Spears was allowed to enter the holy state of marriage for an entire fifty-five hours because she's heterosexual and thus brings honor to the sacred tradition.

MARBLE CEILING

Roll Call's "Heard on the Hill" column reported in January 2007 that Nancy Pelosi, the first-ever female speaker of the House, was also the "first-ever speaker to create a phrase that actually made it into Urban Dictionary." Hopefully she's bookmarked urbandictionary.com.

maxing

Chilling in the best way possible.

I'm just maxin', relaxin', it ain't too taxin'!

mayne

Southern way to say "man." Used in a lot of crunk songs.

What up, mayne?

McBreath

Bad breath caused by eating McDonald's food.

Yo, you got some gum? That Big Mac just gave me some nasty McBreath!

McCulture

Fast-food culture, i.e. lack of culture, in reference to McDonald's. Fatty, uninteresting, nutritionally void, and resembling cardboard in depth and flavor.

Do you blame McCulture for the dumbing down of the public or the dumbing down of the public for McCulture?

McDreamy

A man who is the epitome of charming. A man whose hair is simply uh-mazing. A man who makes the wrong decisions and is often known as an asshole, jerk, or the ultimate heartbreaker. A man, who is none other than the infamous Patrick Dempsey, who plays Dr. Derek Shepherd on the ABC hit series *Grey's Anatomy*.

Dr. Meredith Grey: But that does not change the fact that she's got my McDreamy. And my McDog. She's got my McLife!

Dr. George O'Malley: I think I'm going to McVomit.

McJob

A job, usually in the retail or service sector, that is low paying, often temporary, and offers minimal or no benefits or opportunity for promotion.

We need to expand the skilled job market, not just create more McJobs.

meanderthal

People who wander around aimlessly and always seem to get in your way in stores and supermarkets, chatting on their cell phones and paying no attention to their surroundings.

I would have been here ten minutes earlier if I hadn't been stuck behind that meanderthal.

meatmarket

A place with the sole (stated or unstated) purpose of facilitating interaction of individuals for sexual/romantic activities. The term draws parallels between real meat markets, where meat is hung up and displayed in plain view for people to look at, judge the quality of, and make decisions of whether to buy, and the atmosphere of many nightclubs/

M

bars that are seemingly only in existence so individuals can display themselves to others for judgment and "acquisition," and likewise, size up and attempt to "acquire" others.

Girl 1: We're going down to Elements for some drinks. Wanna come?

Girl 2: Ew, no! That place is such a meatmarket.

media whore

A person who has a psychological need to get into TV, film, radio, or print and becomes aroused almost sexually by seeing or hearing themselves in the media.

Most people who audition for reality TV series or write excessive numbers of letters to the editor are nothing more than media whores.

meh

A way of expressing indifference. The verbal equivalent of a shrug of the shoulders.

Gabe: What do you want for dinner?

Sarah: Meh.

me-mail

A self-centered email, which talks in detail about your weekend, your relationships, or how you are feeling, etc., the contents of which are likely to be irrelevant to its recipients or are written purely as a form of self-therapy. Can be ambiguously

friendly or malicious; within a close-knit group, me-mails may be written to alleviate feelings of status envy in the sender or to attempt to evoke those feelings in its recipients.

Me-mail: Hi guys, had a fantastic weekend. It's going SO well with me and John—I just can't get enough of him! Don't want to pour cold water on it but I think he's going to propose soon! I know I'm so lucky to have met him, and he's so rich, too. We went to the most amazing restaurant on Saturday and then he drove me all the way down the coast just for afternoon tea. How lucky am I?! Can't believe it's Monday already though—still, only a few more days till the weekend!! Can't wait!!!! Janet

mensch

An upstanding, worthy, honorable adult person of either sex.

Be a mensch! Admit your mistake and make things good.

mental masturbation

Intellectual activity that serves no practical purpose.

We debated and created a perfect system of government, but it was all just mental masturbation, really.

mental whiplash

The mental effect of realizing that a basic assumption of your entire life was wrong from day one, usually resulting from a totally new thought, comment, or experience that flies in the face of everything you currently know.

Brace yourself for a mental whiplash, son . . . your mother and I are siblings.

message interruptis
After calling someone you don't want to talk to, you're relieved to hear the familiar sound of their answering machine. You're almost done leaving your perfect getaway message when—Surprise!— you're chatting live because someone picked up the phone after hearing your voice.

I called in sick yesterday and suffered major message interruptis when my boss suddenly picked up the phone.

metawork
Trivial or unnecessary work done to avoid having to perform the real task at hand while simultaneously taking the credit for it. In the business world, metawork often manifests itself in the form of meetings, mission statements, project planning, or anything else that lets a person become part of the team without actually doing something productive.

Eight people were required to complete that project on time, but six of them were only doing metawork. Had it been only the remaining two they would have finished it in half the time.

metrosexual
A straight man who embraces the homosexual lifestyle, e.g., refined tastes in clothing, excessive use of designer hygiene products, etc. Usually is on the brink of homosexuality.

Mike has become a metrosexual after shaving off his stubble and using expensive skin-care products to soften his cherubic facial features.

middle-named
When someone is really mad at you, so they yell your first and middle name.

Mom: Betty Louise, did you make this huge dent in the car door?!

Betty Louise (on the phone): Oh, man, Sara, I just got middle-named.

midnight gardening
The act of passing out or falling over in foliage after large amounts of liquor have been consumed.

He's fine, he's just over in the bushes doing a spot of midnight gardening.

military factor
The factor by which a male's hotness increases when he's in his uniform. On a scale of one to ten, a uniform usually increases a guy's number by two. Can also be applied to non-military men in some uniforms.

Person 1: *Check that guy out. He's a solid seven.*

Person 2: *Him? He's in my Spanish class. He's in AFROTC. On Tuesdays when he's in his dress blues he's a nine, at least. The military factor really helps.*

milkshake

A woman's body and the way she carries it.

Kelis's hit single "Milkshake": My whipped ice dairy drink brings the attention of many males to my place of residence and/or employment, and they declare that its quality far surpasses that of yours. Absolutely, it far surpasses yours. I could convey to you the recipe, but I would have to demand compensation.

mirrorface

The look of coolness, focus, and determination that appears on one's grill when in front of a mirror. A self-preservation technique in which one fantasizes about looking way better than they really do, usually occurring prior to a significant social outing.

Rick got suited up for a night out with his homies. Prior to his departure into the evening, he gave himself one final mirrorface. He knew he was ready to slay some hoes.

mirthquake

An episode of laughter that entails shaking or violent motion.

You should prepare yourselves for a mirthquake, 'cause that movie is really funny.

mob

When a large group of people quickly walks, runs, or drives somewhere.

We mobbed up on that skate park like flies on poop, man!

moded

To put someone in their place after they've been proven wrong.

Man: Hey baby, can I get yo' number?

Woman: No, but you can get lost.

Man's friends: Ooooooh, moded!

moms

An affectionate term for your mother.

I was talking on the phone with my moms.

MONEY

Urban Dictionary has about 1,200 words on the important subject of money. They include "green," "cheddar," "bread," "cheese," "cake," "loot," "dough," "scrilla," "hashish," "coin," "paper," "benjamins," "dead presidents," "Mr. Got Rocks," "FU money," "Kraft singles," and "pockets on swole." Which one do they use on Wall Street?

monitor malaise
When you get sick from looking at a computer monitor.

Shit, man, I gotta go to the other room. I am gettin' mad monitor malaise from bein' in here.

moobs
A combination of the words "man" and "boobs." This is what happens when fat gathers in a male's chest area and gives him the appearance of having breasts. Usually seen in overweight males, but can strangely also occur in men who are not really overweight.

Those moobs are quite sizable. He needs a bra.

mook
A jerk; not a nice person.

That guy just bumped into you and didn't even say sorry. What a mook!

mooninite
Two-dimensional creatures that hail from the inner core of the moon. They are arrogant, are often bad influences on those who come in contact with them, and have the ability to shoot large squarelike projectiles from their moon weapons. They can be seen on the Adult Swim show *Aqua Teen Hunger Force*. Mooninites launched an attack on Earth in January 2007. They succeeded in shutting down Boston on Wednesday, January 31.

We are the mooninites from the inner core of the moon.

moose knuckle
The male version of a camel toe. Usually found on older rotund gentlemen wearing a suit.

That guy in the business meeting was so big, his moose knuckle looked like a fanny pack gone wrong.

MoPro
Short for "mobile professional." Mobile professionals are white-collar workers who spend at least 50 percent of their work hours away from their main office. Mobile professionals are often characterized by crackberry addiction, high divorce rate, pearly whites, and inflated titles like "emerging technology strategist."

My boss is a MoPro, so I spend most of my time browsing MySpace.

more cowbell
Something everything needs more of; a remedy. From a popular sketch on *Saturday Night Live* featuring Christopher Walken as Bruce Dickinson.

Bruce Dickinson: I got a fever and the only prescription is more cowbell.

Mormon assault vehicle
A station wagon, minivan, or any other kind of vehicle that is targeted at the "family" demographic. Also: "M.A.V."

M

Tactical advantages aside, the M.A.V. is the top of the line of holy warrior troop transport manufactured by the Church of Latter Day Saints Military Industrial Complex. Also great for family trips . . . to heathen lands.

mosh

A way of expressing yourself at a metal rock/punk concert by jumping up and down, crowd surfing, and just generally going crazy. You get pushed around and shoved, and you fall on your ass, but it's all in the spirit of a great time. Almost always done in a "pit" with extremely cool people whom you don't even know but who will look out for you.

A concert isn't a concert without moshing in a pit!

move units

To make moves; do big things; sell.

Since last year 50 Cent has really been movin' units!

MRS degree

The ultimate goal of some women who enroll in college: to find a suitable husband.

She's only here to get her MRS degree.

muffin top

When a woman wears a pair of tight jeans that makes her flab spill out over the waistband, just like the top of a muffin sits over the edge of the paper case.

Sweet Jesus! Look at the muffin top on that deuce.

mullet ratio

A mathematical term used to describe how extreme a mullet hairstyle is. It is found by comparing how long the hair on top of the head is compared to how long the hair hangs at the back of the neck.

My mullet ratio is a half inch on top and sixteen inches at the back. It's bitchin'!

multiculti

A person who is multiracial.

Frank is a fine-looking multiculti brotha!

multislacking

Doing multiple slackeresque things concurrently.

I'm the king of multislacking. I spend hours a day surfing the 'net, watching random TV shows, and eating week-old pizza.

multitasking

A polite way of telling someone you haven't heard a word they said. Commonly used on long conference calls, when the speaker is monotonous, boring, or couldn't make a point if one were drawn for him.

Joe: Blah, blah corporate office blah, blah, leverage proactively blah, blah human capital and grade-A synergy, blah, blah.

Do you agree, Jim?

Jim: I'm sorry, Joe, I was multitasking, can you repeat that?

murse
A man purse.

Nice murse, Frank!

muscle queen
A gay man who pumps iron every waking moment in order to be as physically appealing to other men as possible.

I found a great apartment on 23rd and 7th—immaculate, pine wood floors, rent control, and best of all, my new roommate's never home; he spends all his time at David Barton Gym. Total muscle queen.

music ADD
Music attention deficit disorder. You can't find a good song to listen to. You might find one you like but about thirty seconds into the song you're sick of it and skip it.

Person 1: Man, I can't find anything to listen to.

Person 2: You must have music ADD.

Person 1: I need new music.

musk up
To apply cologne to a man's body.

We're hittin' the clubs tonight. Time to musk up.

musterbate
To sit idly and think.

That is a lot of money. I will have to musterbate for a while before I make a decision.

MySpace face
The face everyone makes in their MySpace pictures. Girls: pouty eyes with a smirk or pursed lips. The shoulder comes up and attaches to the chin. Fingers in the west side sign optional. For guys: shirt up showing off their abs while making some macho head nod, face looking cool and unassuming.

Matt: Damn, did you see Mikayla's MySpace?

Mario: Yeah, she's got that MySpace face, right?

MySpaceing out
When you spend hours upon end looking at others' MySpace profiles and commenting.

Person 1: Why were you late for work today?

M

Person 2: I was on my computer for three hours MySpaceing out, and then I looked at the time and had to rush to work.

Urban Dictionary receives about 1,700 submissions a day. If it takes about thirty seconds to read an entry and decide whether it should be published, that's more than a day's worth of work for one person! Fortunately, many volunteer editors review the newest definitions and decide whether each one should be published. Since editors began reviewing content on the site in March 2005, over 130,000 people have helped review newly submitted definitions.

mysterectomy

Taking all the suspense out of a movie by revealing spoilers to someone who hasn't seen it.

Person 1: What are you watching?

Person 2: The Village. I haven't seen it yet.

Person 1: Cool . . . you know it's set in the present, right?

Person 2: Oh, goddammit! Thanks for the mysterectomy!

myspy

When you use MySpace to spy on ex-boyfriends, ex-girlfriends, ex-friends, or even your ex-boyfriend's ex-girlfriend's ex-boyfriend's baby mama.

My boyfriend caught me myspying on my ex-boyfriend's ex-girlfriend. Busted.

mo'urban

nametake

The reverse of namesake; a person you are named after.

The monk Martin Luther was the nametake of Dr. King.

nap fraud

When one pretends to sleep for any reason, possibly so they don't have to do something, to get attention, or to find out gossip and secrets. Very useful for finding out information you might not be supposed to know.

Penny: No no, it's OK, Andrew's sleeping.

Jenny: OK. Well, I really like Andrew's dad. He's really sexy.

Penny: Cool. I think I might have a thing for my uncle. Probably just a phase!

Jenny: God, Penny! Andrew's not really sleeping! He's committing nap fraud.

naplash

What happens to you when you start nodding off and then you jerk your head back suddenly. Happens a lot when staying on the computer too long. Very dangerous if driving.

If you didn't get enough sleep, and you're driving, please pull over at the first instance of naplash. If possible, get coffee or walk around, or take a proper nap.

nappy-headed ho

According to Don Imus, a female basketball player at Rutgers University. This caused CBS and NBC to fire Imus.

They got tattoos; those are some nappy-headed hos.

nastygram

Letter sent to an individual or organization in professional "business-angry" style, expressing displeasure about actions taken, or lack thereof.

I sent a nastygram to my cell phone provider regarding why they've not adjusted my account, and they were pretty quick to fix it after that.

natch
Abbreviation for "naturally."

I am a member. So I went to the meeting, natch.

National Hangover Day
New Year's Day; the aftermath of hard drinking and partying on New Year's Eve.

I woke up next to five bottles of Jägermeister and a pile of confetti on National Hangover Day.

natty
"Good," "cool," or "elite"; originates from Rastafarian culture.

Hey, natty dreads, mon.

naughties
The 2000s decade, as "nineties" or "eighties" are used in reference to their respective decades.

Hey, do you remember the naughties?

NCMO
Acronym for "Noncommittal make out."

Yo, he just got some NCMO from butterface.

necro
To bring back something dead; often used in reference to topics in online forums.

I thought this thread was history, but someone necro'd it by bumping on it.

nekkid
Gettin' naked for mischievous purposes. "Naked" is natural; "nekkid" is naughty.

Come over quick, Shirley! I'm getting nekkid!

nerdrection
When a nerd experiences or anticipates a certain event that is expected to have a positive effect.

When members of my cast heard you were coming on my show, they received a nerdrection.

New Ageist
Used to describe individuals who discriminate against others who are not overly focused on self-improvement. Such people often look down on people who do not practice yoga, eat organic, and believe in energy fields.

My date last night was a disaster because the guy is completely New Ageist. He is seriously opposed to dating girls who are not into meditation and eating sprouts.

New York minute

An instant. Or as Johnny Carson once said, it's the interval between a Manhattan traffic light turning green and the guy behind you honking his horn. A reference to the frenzied and hectic pace of New Yorkers' lives.

I'll have that ready for you in a New York minute.

nextflix

The upcoming movies in your Netflix queue.

My two nextflix are due to arrive on Wednesday.

NFG

Military acronym for "no fucking good."

This equipment is NFG.

NIB

Acronym for "new in box." Brand new and never used.

I saw a few NIB items up on eBay last night.

nickel bag

A $5 sack of weed; enough for one joint.

My little brother: Got any weed?

Me: I got a nickel bag, and no you can't have any.

nicotini

An alcoholic drink that includes nicotine as an ingredient; usually made with vodka in which tobacco has been soaked. Generally billed as an alternative for smokers in smoke-free establishments.

After the city-wide smoking ban came into effect, my only option was to drink an occasional nicotini while barhopping.

Nike defense

Running away from a violent confrontation, particularly using Nike sports shoes.

We was running low on ammo, so we used the Nike defense and hauled ass outta there.

ninja sex

Having noiseless sex (no squeaking springs or vocals) while one or more people are passed out in the same room.

N

Lil B was drunk and passed out in our room. We were horny, so we had ninja sex.

nintendonitis

A chronic painful condition that affects the muscles or joints in the hand, fingers, and/or forearm after playing video games too much.

Dude, I played Final Fantasy for three days straight, but my nintendonitis flared up so I couldn't play anymore.

nipplegate

The scandal of the 2004 Super Bowl halftime show in which Janet Jackson accidentally exposed her entire right breast.

Nipplegate provoked a media frenzy.

nod of acknowledgment

The nod of acknowldgement is a standard among guys as a way to let the person know that you see them, without having to resort to using words. Girls will generally not accept the nod of acknowledgment and opt for a wave of the hand and/or a smile, perhaps even accompanied by words. The nod of acknowledgment is a wordless conversation. The only acceptable response to a nod of acknowledgment is another nod. If you speak, you have broken the point of such a gesture.

Situations in which the nod of acknowledgment may be used:

Walking past a friend to class

Catching a friend's eye across the room to say hi without verbally saying it

Giving approval of a friend's actions

no homo

Phrase used after one inadvertently says something that sounds gay.

His ass is mine. No homo.

noids

Paranoia.

Man, that pot brownie gave me some serious noids!

nonpology

An insincere apology or expression of regret, often blaming the aggrieved party for being offended or bringing up an irrelevant topic to distract.

NONPOLOGY

Don Imus's comments in April 2007 led to his dismissal at CBS. His apology, in which he pointed out that rap artists frequently use the same terms and aren't dismissed, became Urban Dictionary's canonical example for "nonpology." The incident also generated new definitions of "nappy-headed ho": "According to Don Imus, a female basketball player at Rutgers University."

Did you hear Don Imus's nonpology the other day? Like his racist remarks are actually the result of rap music.

nontourage

A group of undesirable sycophants.

The party was fun until Chris showed up with his nontourage.

nooner

Sex done at lunch, your lunch break, or around noon. Used by Al Bundy of *Married with Children*.

Nooners rock.

nose goes

A way of determining who has to do a task, such as close a door or turn off a light after everyone is seated. To call "nose goes," you simply place your index finger on your nose, and say "nose goes." The last person to call "nose goes" has to do the task.

Amber: Someone turn off the light, it's putting a glare on the TV.

Everyone but Julia: Nose goes.

Julia: Aww, you guys suck.

nosh

To snack.

Stop your noshin' or you won't want to eat dinner.

note to crowd

A phrase used to attract attention to a fact or piece of information to the room at large. Similar to "note to self," except that it serves as a reminder/informer of information to a group of people instead of the speaker alone.

Note to crowd: It's Danny's round.

note to self

1. An exclamation used when you want to punctuate/emphasize an obvious or insulting quip or action.

Note to self: Jared is an idiot!

2. An exclamation highlighting something you did not know until then.

Note to self: Don't put wooden objects in the dishwasher.

3. A personal reminder.

Note to self: Pay rent.

NSFS

Acronym for "not safe for school." Used to describe Internet content generally inappropriate for school, i.e., would not be acceptable in the presence of a teacher or principal.

Guys, check this site out. Careful, though, its NSFS.

N

NSFW

Acronym for "not safe for work."
Also "NWS," "not work safe."

*These pictures of Britney Spears getting out
of her car are NSFW.*

number four year

A year whose number is divisible by
four in which most events that operate on a four-year cycle take place,
such as leap year, Summer Olympics,
and the United States presidential
election.

Y2K was one hectic number four year.

O

obliviot

An oblivious idiot.

At the store, this total obliviot stopped in the middle of the aisle, blocking the way with his cart so nobody could get past.

OCT

An acronym for "on company time." The time when most Americans pay their bills, catch up with loved ones via email, make weekend plans, pur-

> OCT is closely related to "Internet anytime minutes," which are the minutes (that add up to hours) that you spend surfing the Internet at work. Also see "casual undertime."

chase plane tickets and eBay items, and spend most of their restroom time during the day.

We were playing Pong OCT!

October surprise

An unexpected, dramatic last-minute event that potentially alters the outcome of an election. The term dates to the 1980 presidential campaign, in which Jimmy Carter planned, for October of that year, an operation to rescue American hostages held in Iran. Carter was lagging behind in polls and a successful rescue, an "October surprise," would likely have shifted the momentum to his side. The attempt failed, however, and Carter lost the election. Some have suggested that the Reagan campaign deliberately sabotaged the effort in order to bolster his candidacy.

Before Osama bin Laden released his newest tape, some people thought the Bush campaign would produce him as an October surprise.

O face

A term used in the movie *Office Space* to describe the face one makes when achieving orgasm.

I'm gonna be showing her my O face.

off the chain

1. A great deal of fun.

Wow, Mike, this party has punch and cake and everything! It's really off the chain!

2. Very attractive.

That girl has a nice rack. She is off the chain.

off the reservation

Crazy.

I'm terrified of this girl. She's completely off the reservation.

oh-shit bar

The handle found in most cars to either hold onto around corners taken at speed, or to hang shirts and such. Also called the "oh-shit handle."

Dude, you better grab the oh-shit bar!

oh, what now

1. Something to say after being insulted/insulting someone.

Dude 1 (to innocent bystander): Your mom!

Dude 2: Oh, what now!

2. Something to yell out randomly.

Dude 1: I saw your mom at Wally World shopping for your birthday present!

Dude 2: Oh, what now!

3. Something to say when you don't understand something. Usually follows "your face" and "your mom."

Dude 1: Yeah, your face is so gay it takes three trucks!

Dude 2: Oh, what now?

.old

When you link someone to a web site they have already seen. It refers to a fictional top-level domain (like .com, .net, and .edu) that, if it existed, would house all the old shit everyone has seen.

Guy 1: Have you seen tubgirl?

Guy 2: You mean www.tubgirl.old?

omega male

Male in a group who is least likely to take the initiative and lead, due to a lack of self-esteem, ability, or interest. Opposite of "alpha male."

I'm going to break routine and lead this project. I'm tired of being the omega male.

one-cheek sneak

The act of quietly squeezing out a fart when sitting down by leaning to the side slightly and raising one cheek.

My girlfriend always knows when I fart because, even though I do the one-cheek sneak, I always give it away with my farting facial expression.

one-eyed

Drunk to the point where you have to close one eye to avoid double vision.

I feel like shit. Me and a buddy went out and got one-eyed last night.

oneitis

The dreaded ailment of liking that "one special girl" and wanting her more than any other woman on earth. A want so intense that it's actually painful.

Man, don't waste your time talking to Aaron. He's got oneitis for Becky.

one love

The universal love and respect expressed by all people for all people, regardless of race, creed, or color.

It's all good. One love.

one putt

Task that is expected to be relatively easy but, if not done properly, can turn into an embarrassing nightmare.

CBS executives: Here's the latest on the Bush Air National Guard story. The docs show Bush's superiors thought he was a schmuck, too. This is a one-putt story if I've ever seen one—run it tonight at 6:00.

onion booty

Booty that looks so good, it makes a grown man want to cry.

Damn, man, that girl's got onion booty.

on tilt

To gamble recklessly and aggressively after a bad or improbable bet or series of bad or improbable bets. Usually results in losing all of your money and then some. Good gamblers avoid this at all costs, even if it means going home earlier than expected.

After he got beat three straight times, Mike went on tilt and got his whole bankroll taken.

organically overlap

Term used by New Age and/or granola types to describe an accidental meeting or spending time together without previously having made a plan.

I have yoga later, but we will probably organically overlap at one of the Greenpeace meetings.

orly

Internet term meaning "Oh, really?" Can also be used with "no wai" (no way) and "ya rly" (yes, really).

Her: i'm pregnant.

Me: orly

Her: yarly

outercourse

Dry humping. Some people prefer this since there is no direct skin-to-skin contact, meaning no STDs or pregnancy.

Outercourse is t3h sex.

out of pocket

To be out of control; way off base. Usually deserving of a good slapping or a full-blown ass-kicking.

Tamika had seven shots of Hennessy last night and tried to get on my man. She was way out of pocket, so I smacked the belligerent ho.

outside

It's uncomfortable and there's this big hot thing in the sky and there are other people you sometimes have to talk to.

I don't want to go outside.

out the cuts

Out of nowhere; when someone/something appears suddenly without announcement.

Shelly: When did Carson get here? I didn't even see him come in.

Kodi: Yeah, he just came out the cuts like, "What's up, guys, where's the party?"

overshare

Too much information, or "TMI."

Mom: Did I ever tell you about how you were conceived?

Me: Uh, no, Mom, that would be an overshare.

overvite

An invite that occurs after another invite has already been extended.

Jeff: I would have people over to watch hockey at my place, but I don't want to overvite Josh's party.

Daniel: True, but I would rather go to your place any day.

own

To wear clothing, accessories, or physical features with confidence.

I was a little nervous about wearing such skimpy trousers, but I decided I just gotta own that shit.

Pac-Manning

To drive right on the dotted white lane divider, which gives the same effect as Pac-Man eating dots.

Dude, quit Pac-Manning. You're gonna hit that car.

Pac-Manning is also known as "driving by Braille." Maybe you've driven home this way and didn't know what to call it—one blogger commented that Urban Dictionary's best definitions "show examples of things you know and have seen, but have never identified."

PAC-MANNING

ud

padded-furniture generation

The generation of children whose parents protect them from everything.

John: Hey, Stephen, is that kid on a leash?

Stephen: Yup. He's a victim of the padded-furniture generation.

paid witness

An unarmed security guard. (What the hell is this guy gonna do against a heat-packing thief?)

Lady: Aahhh! That guy just took my purse!

Guard: He sure did!

Lady: Well, do something, dammit!

Guard: What do you want me to do? Run up and slap him so he can knife me to death?

Lady: You're nothing but a paid witness!

pancake

1. To end a relationship suddenly.

It's time to pancake Jim.

2. To get dumped by someone and remain clueless to the reason.

I got pancaked.

paper
Money.

I'll take that paper.

paperview
A method of finding out the results or information of a favorite sports team or TV show by reading about it in the newspaper.

Man, I forgot to pay my cable bill last month, so now I have to rely on paperview to see if my team's winning.

parade wave
A slight hand gesture used to wave for prolonged periods of time (like during a parade) or as a casual nonverbal greeting to friends. With the arm bent at the elbow, the waver turns their wrist back and forth exposing the front and then the back of the hand in a single motion.

I didn't feel like talking so I gave her a quick parade wave as I walked by.

parentnoia
The irrational fear parents have that their children are doing something wrong or being hurt in some way.

Any time Jenny went on a date her father was filled with parentnoia.

park in goofy
When you park your car in a very large parking lot and have to practically take a tram to get back to it. Each section of the parking lot at Walt Disney World is labeled by character names, and Goofy is the section farthest from the ticket center. Similar to "BFE."

Yeah, I got to school late again. I'm parked in goofy for the third time this week.

party foul
Something socially unacceptable done in a social gathering.

Kelly knocked his beer out of his hand. What a party foul.

party promise
Plans you make at the end of social gatherings where one, if not both, promisers never actually intend to follow through.

Kelsey: Dude, we should totally grab coffee sometime soon!

Brianna: Yeah, totally!

(One or both is thinking: This coffee date will never happen, but I can stop talking to them now.)

party socks
Socks not removed prior to intercourse. Said socks need not be used only during sex. Party socks are usually the result of laziness or haste.

*We were totally going at it but I had to
stop him because I couldn't stop laughing
at his party socks.*

patriotourism
The act of visiting a place as a tourist to help in the recovery of that
place from a disaster.

*The most recent example of patriotourism
is post-Katrina New Orleans, where people
have been coming from around the world to
bolster the local economy.*

PCV
Acronym for "penis compensation
vehicle." A vehicle altered to make
a cowardly driver feel bigger than
he really is, usually with lift kits, bull
testicles, winches, and various off-
road accessories that will likely never
be used off-road. Often but not
limited to pickup trucks and sport
utility vehicles.

*I got cut off by some teenager in a PCV,
but he ran inside crying to his parents when
I tried to confront him.*

PDQ
Acronym for "pretty damn quick."
Faster than "ASAP."

I need the money PDQ.

pedestrian face-off
An awkward situation in which two
pedestrians on a collision course
with each other are repeatedly
unsuccessful in avoiding one
another. As one person moves to
their right, the other person moves
to their left and vice versa. Each
time they attempt a new maneuver,
the frustrated pedestrians find
themselves confronted by their
counterpart. To the casual observer,
these two people may appear to be
dancing, but in reality, they both just
want to get on with their lives.

*I just had a pedestrian face-off that lasted
a good fifteen seconds. In the end, we came
to the mutual agreement that both of us
should step to our right.*

peegasm
The euphoric shiver felt by the
human male during a long-awaited
urination.

*I had such a violent peegasm I pissed all
over the leg of the guy next to me, and he
subsequently proceeded to beat the shit out
of me. But wow, what a peegasm.*

peeps
Marshmallow candies in the shape
of rabbits, baby chickens, and other
holiday symbols. Started with Easter.
Also short for "people."

*I'm audi this Sunday to chill with some
peeps.*

pee shy

The inability to urinate in public.

Guy 1: What's the matter? I thought you said you had to go?

Guy 2: I do, but I just got pee shy.

penis sympathy

The feeling of vicarious pain most men feel when they hear of another man in a situation in which his penis has been injured.

Hey, Jack, remember the end of that fishing trip when the car trunk accidentally slammed down on Phil's crotch? Man, I couldn't have sex for days after that one.

percussive maintenance

Bludgeoning an electronic device to encourage it to work properly. Vigorous beatings often render the device permanently nonfunctional.

My goddamned monitor was flickering until I used some percussive maintenance; now it's totally dead and Help Desk is bringing me a new one.

period of great unknown

A point of exploration in a relationship in which one does not know whether they want to be with their partner anymore. A less harsh way to say "a break." Allows for a doubter to make out with other boys.

Girl: I don't think I'll be able to trust you anymore.

Guy: Are we breaking up?

Girl: Not really. We're just in a period of great unknown.

perma-stoned

The condition of being permanently stoned from smoking marijuana constantly. Those with this condition are often accused of being stoned even when they are sober.

Aaron hits the weed at least four times a day. The kid's perma-stoned.

perma-sweater

No shirt, no problem, because you're wearing a sweater of body hair year-round.

Bryan looked hot at the beach, in part because of his perma-sweater.

perp walk

Practice of displaying an arrested person to the press and public while delivering the person to the courtroom, etc.

Giuliani arrested stockbrokers and took them on a perp walk, when he could have arranged for them to surrender quietly.

PHB

Acronym for "Pointy Haired Boss" as featured in the long running *Dilbert* cartoon strip by Scott Adams. The phrase suggests an office manager with above-average incompetence, general cluelessness, and an ability to prevent anyone else in the office from doing any useful work. Actual pointy hair is not a requirement for PHBs, but there is strong anecdotal evidence that they will rapidly develop the distinctive hairstyle.

My PHB asked me if the firewall was a serious fire hazard.

phlog

Fake blog; a web site pretending to be a blog but actually the creation of the mainstream media or professional political operatives.

Talon News was a phlog created to grab the focus from real blogs and insert government spin into the online community.

phone stamina

The total amount of time one can manage being on the phone with someone.

My phone stamina is roughly an hour.

Picasso pause

When a person stands still for a moment admiring their own work.

That guy wouldn't have gotten hurt if he wasn't standing there doing his Picasso pause when the building collapsed.

pi day

March 14. A "holiday" celebrated by math geeks everywhere. Pi is approximately 3.14, and March 14 is 3/14.

omg t3h pi day d00d, we are so 1337, pi roxxors t3h boxxors!

piglet

A police officer in training.

Check out that piglet!

pimp daddy

Cool guy who has a fly ride and can get bitches and weed in less than an hour.

Hey, pimp daddy, I gotz to get crunked tonight. Can you hook it up?

pimposterous

Unbelievably smooth.

His outfit is totally pimposterous!

piss in the wind

To do something that is a complete waste of effort and time. You can expect no results and it may even backfire on you.

It's pissing in the wind to tell the president that invading other countries is unpopular with many voters.

pitted out

Long past the working time of your deodorant, when you start to get

BO and the armpits of your shirt get wet.

I'm all pitted out after that two-hour meeting. It was so hot!

pityplause

The applause one receives out of pity despite a poor performance.

Despite stumbling over her lines, the comedienne received a round of pityplause from her audience.

plane name

The name you use to identify yourself to the stranger sitting next to you on the plane.

Man, I just flew in from the West Coast sitting next to this wacko—thank god I used my plane name or else I'd be worried about him stalking me.

play ahab

To search for a specific elusive something. In reference to the *Moby Dick* character who relentlessly pursued the white whale, which is a metaphor for the unattainable or what the searcher believes to be perfect.

Forget her. I'm living in the ocean and I refuse to play ahab.

played out

Old, boring, cliché.

That music's played out.

player

A male who is skilled at manipulating ("playing") others, and especially at seducing women by pretending to care about them, when in reality he is only interested in sex. Possibly derived from the phrases "play him for a fool," or "play him like a violin."

Gina thought she had found the love of her life when she met Sean, but after she found out he had slept with three of her best friends, she realized that he was nothing but a player.

playlistism

Discrimination based not on race, sex, or religion, but rather on a disturbingly horrible iTunes music library discovered through a school or job network. Refers to the "shared music" feature available on iTunes in which one can browse the various music libraries of nearby computers. Often requires awkward explanation of why you have "that song."

Mike accused me of playlistism when I questioned his collection of Color Me Badd b-sides.

pluto

To downgrade, demote, or remove altogether from a prestigious group or list, like what was done to the planet Pluto.

He was plutoed like an old pair of shoes.

POATEW

Acronym for "pissed off at the entire world."

After Darrell got a second speeding ticket in the same day, he was POATEW for the rest of the week.

pobody's nerfect

Another way of saying, "nobody's perfect." Used by *Cracked* and *Mad* magazine in the 1970s.

Girl: I'm sorry, that was dumb.

Guy: That's okay, pobody's nerfect.

pod snob

Someone who continuously listens to his or her iPod, unable to detect being spoken to, and is unaware of any other conversation taking place around him or her.

Gina: Right, David? . . . David!

Emily: He can't hear you; he's being a pod snob.

polish a turd

The act of trying to make something hopelessly weak and unattractive appear strong and appealing. An impossible process that usually results in a larger, uglier turd.

She tried to look more attractive by getting plastic surgery, but let's face it, you can't polish a turd.

poopin'

Doing well, rockin', beating everyone else.

Our school's basketball team is poopin'.

pop hundies

To spend big bills, such as hundred-dollar bills.

Donald Trump is so damn rich. That bastard is always poppin' hundies.

pop off

To tell someone to fight you or do something, rather than just standing there talking about it.

Bob: Shut up before I punch you in your face.

You: What?! U so hard then pop off!

poppin' fresh

Extremely fresh.

You look poppin' fresh, homie!

porch dog

A person who frequently attacks others in speech or writing but who poses no intellectual threat. This type of person is usually obnoxious and offensive. Refers to dogs that sit on front porches and bark vigorously and fruitlessly at passersby but pose no physical threat.

Yeah, that guy has a scathing response to just about everyone who posts in this forum. He's a real porch dog.

P

porn groove

The awesome music in a porno. Tacky and delightful. Sounds like "untz" or "bow chicka WOW wow."

Dude, this porn groove is classic.

pornfolio

The mass of porn that one has stored on their computer.

Damn, dude, I got 117 porn mpegs in my pornfolio.

posse

Your crew, your homies, a group of friends; people who have your back.

Me an' my posse gonna hang tonight.

post up

To chill or stand at a spot (like a club or a street corner, etc). To claim a spot. The term came from drug dealers on street corners, like light posts and street posts.

Urban Dictionary has about nine hundred words that are related to "pot." It's an important subject—here are some of the top related words: "weed," "bud," "ganja," "Mary Jane," "hydro," "spliff," "Buddha," "cheeba," "MJ," "doobie," "sticky icky," "nug," "tree," "chronic," "green," "herb," "kind bud," "wacky tabacky," and "maui wowie."

Yo, let's post up right there where all the honeys with the big booties are.

pot commit

In poker, to bet so much that you have put the majority of your chips in play, leaving very little in reserve should you lose the hand.

After being dealt big slick, Rob pot committed himself pre-flop, and when nothing hit, he was left with a decision of going all-in or checking.

POTUS

Acronym for "president of the United States."

Ronald Reagan was the fortieth POTUS.

prairie dog

When people's heads pop up over the walls in a cube farm to see what's going on.

What's with everyone prairie dogging when I scream here?!

prayer

Although not promoted by public schools, it is the most popular study technique of high school students, typically used minutes before a test.

OK, study time. Please, please let me pass this test . . .

precreate

To procreate for recreation.

We were bored and decided to spend the day watching porn in order to precreate.

pregame
To drink before going to a party, most often because the party will be carding and you are underage or because you want to drink something hard to start your night off. Often happens at a house and involves shots.

We really need to pregame tonight before we go out.

pregret
The feeling of regretting something you know you will inevitably do anyway.

Every Friday night, I pregret that I will go to the club. I know I will stand there like an idiot and won't talk enough game to bring anyone home with me.

pre-pull
To pull the car door handle at the moment the driver unlocks the door, rendering the attempt fruitless and resulting in minor frustration and/or embarrassment.

Could you unlock it again, dude? I pre-pulled.

presidential tint
The darkest tint you can have on a car's windows. Most cars that have it are ridin' dirty, so if you have it, cops will give you tickets to harass you.

You know I ride with that presidential tint . . . but I ride clean, busta.

PRETEXTING

Pretexting is the new business euphemism for flat-out lying. Doesn't sound so bad, does it? You could almost hire a Chief of Pretexting. *ud*

pretexting
Euphemism for lying. Calling a telephone company or a financial institution and obtaining sensitive, personal information about a customer by deceiving the company into believing that you are that customer.

It was revealed that Hewlett Packard was spying on its board of directors and hired lawyers to obtain information on personal phone calls. The lawyers used pretexting to trick phone companies into releasing that information.

prewalk
To position oneself on a subway platform such that, when the passenger steps off the train at his destination, he'll be as close as possible to the exit or stairs to his transfer. Used and done often in the NYC subway system.

Sorry, I can't talk with you while we wait for the train. I've got to prewalk to the end of the platform.

P

procrastishower

The superlong shower one takes when they have something better to do, like study for a chemistry exam.

I procrastishowered for a whole hour the night before my CHEM 247 term test.

professional celebrity

A famous person who has no discernable talent other than being famous.

Paris Hilton is a professional celebrity.

promosexual

People, usually celebrities, who publicly identify with a currently trendy or rare sexual orientation purely to win attention and admiration.

Britney Spears is such a promosexual.

prosecutie

An attractive female who is below the age of consent.

Emma Watson may be a prosecutie, but she'd be worth the fifteen to twenty hard time.

the pull back

When you go in to kiss a girl and she pulls back in disgust.

When I went in to put one on her, she gave me the pull back and we haven't spoken since.

pull shades

An attempt to conceal an indiscretion, as in pulling down a window shade so no one can see inside.

No you won't pull shades, Miss Thing! (Said to a woman on a diet who was caught sneaking chocolate.)

pulling shirt

A garment to which you are particularly attached due to its acting as something of a lucky charm when it comes to wooing (pulling) the opposite sex.

I get lucky almost every time I wear my pulling shirt.

punk out

To be intimidated to the point of retreat.

Come on, man, jump. Don't punk out.

purple state

A term that is used to describe an even split in a state between Democrat and Republican voters.

Ohio is usually a purple state in presidential elections.

push on

To get on with life, even through hard times.

After we broke up, I had to tell him to push on.

pushing prize

A gift for a new mother, typically an expensive piece of jewelry. "Pushing" refers to the labor of childbirth.

She got a diamond ring as a pushing prize!

pythonate

To be engorged by the consumption of a large, rich, or heavy meal so that you must recline while the meal digests.

The entire family had to pythonate for hours after the Thanksgiving meal.

P

Q

QLC

Acronym for "que la chinga." In Spanish, "que" means "what," "la" means "the," and "chinga" means "fuck." QLC is like WTF. The phrase actually doesn't mean anything in Spanish, but it's good to use when you can't say WTF, like at work.

QLC, man, the store closed like an hour ago and that customer's still in here. I wanna get outta here.

quarter-life crisis

The Diet Pepsi of chronological crises encountered on one's twenty-fifth birthday. Subject often realizes that he or she has lived a quarter century and still hasn't done anything consequential. Subject often buys some time to regroup by getting a McJob.

I think Roger is going through a quarter-life crisis. He's been talking about going back to college so he can actually get a real job someday.

quote criminal

A person who doesn't think of their own jokes and instead repeats funny lines from popular comedies. Quote criminality heavily coincides with overuse of the Internet and too many stacks of DVDs in the perp's apartment. Dave Chappelle, *Family Guy, Napoleon Dynamite,* Ali G., and Monty Python are all regular tools of the quote criminal.

I left the party because these quote criminals got drunk and started acting out entire Monty Python routines. Ugh!

mo'urban

raincoat

A condom.

Always remember your raincoat!

ramen budget

A euphemism for being poor. As ramen can be obtained for a paltry ten cents a pack, it is widely regarded as the single cheapest meal a human can consume.

Guy 1: Hey, man, want to go to the movies tonight?

Guy 2: Can't. I'm on a ramen budget.

rankism

The abuse of the power inherent in superior rank. Rank-based abuse upholds many other forms of discrimination, such as racism, sexism, and homophobia.

The principal ignores input from teachers because he's blinded by rankism.

rasterbator

A person who spends too much time on the Internet or on the computer in general.

Damnit, he's been on Newgrounds all day. He is such a rasterbator.

reality chatspeak

When you chat online for so long that you begin to use phrases like "rofl" and "wtf" in the real world. Also called "chat syndrome."

Sane person: George Bush is a whore.

Dude: rofl!

rebellionaire

Any person who makes his millions off of marketing rebellion or angst.

dictionary

All that crap they package and sell as "alternative" or "punk" these days is just the rebellionaires cashing in.

rebooty

A booty call made with an ex; a renewed relationship with an ex.

After they broke up, Kevin still called Britney for some rebooty on weekends.

re-cop

To acquire more of or to replenish the supply of a particular drug.

Dope is running low. I'm gonna need to re-cop tonight before I'm completely out.

recrunkulous

Ridiculous in the crunkest of ways.

Tommy, that was the most recrunkulous shit you've ever said.

redneck car alarm

Three junkyard dogs sitting in your car with the windows open.

Ever since I got a redneck car alarm, nobody has stolen my stereo.

reefy

Cool or awesome. Often preceded by "so" and used by surfers.

Isaac is so reefy.

refrigerator rights

Defines the depth, closeness, and intimacy of a relationship. Friends with refrigerator rights can help themselves to anything in your refrigerator without asking permission.

Steve and I are so tight, I have refrigerator rights at his place.

regift

To repackage or rewrap a gift one receives and give it to someone else.

Elaine gave Tim a label maker for Christmas—and he regifted it to Jerry!

relationshit

A relationship with a significant other that has gone sour and both parties are too scared and/or lazy to call it quits.

I'm stuck in a crappy relationshit with Jenny.

religiot

Someone who has become so deluded, ignorant, or intolerant in their religious beliefs that they have actually decreased their IQ. Combination of "religion" and "idiot."

The religiot said that homosexuals will cause the apocalypse.

remail

Attempting to follow up on previous email messages that have gone unanswered.

Employee: Jim isn't responding to my email requests to shut down the Hope Creek nuclear power plant before the east shore of New Jersey is a radioactive wasteland.

Boss: Well, remail him. Maybe he's just busy.

resolutionary

People who join a gym after the New Year, only to quit going within three months.

I couldn't find a free treadmill. The place was crawling with resolutionaries.

retail therapy

Shopping as an outlet for frustration and a reliever of stress.

Juju's retail therapy session went quite well; she visited the local Sephora for her fix of new eye shadows, as well as the jewelry cart for a pair of new obnoxious but cute earrings. Nothing beats spending money to forget about your troubles.

retox

To start consuming drugs and alcohol again after a hiatus in an effort to avoid the effects of withdrawal.

Man, I haven't had a drink since Monday and I'm getting the shakes. I'd better retox.

retrograde revolution

The theory that history and culture (e.g. fashion, music, etc.) repeat themselves every couple of decades.

There are many similarities between the war in Iraq today and the Vietnam War. It's almost like a retrograde revolution.

rewind

In the drum and bass scene, the DJ's practice of replaying a record that has been enthusiastically received by the audience. Spectators "call for a rewind" by holding cigarette lighters in the air; if there is enough demand, the DJ will spin the record backward and play it from the beginning.

The crowd loved that track so much that I had to do three rewinds.

ride

A vehicle or mode of transportation; usually belongs to someone else.

Let's use Jesse's ride. It's got room and an a/c.

ride clean

To operate a vehicle without illegal substances. The opposite of "riding dirty." Used by rapper Project Pat.

Lucky for that pig who pulled me over, I decided to ride clean today and didn't have to spark metal on his fat donut-gruffling ass.

ride dirty

To travel in a vehicle with a felonious amount of substance.

Ray-Ray, he ride dirty. Homey had six ounces up in the Escalade.

R

ride neons

To be riding in a car equipped with neon lights on the rims or under-carriage of the car.

Last weekend we rolled around town riding neons on my new whip.

ride on

In the vernacular of mountain biking: "right on," "continue on," "you are doing well," "cool," etc.

Snowflake: Dude, I just cleaned that technical section.

Mike: Ride on!

ringtone DJ

A person who shuffles through all their ringtones, one after another, annoying the people around them. You can yell at them, but they don't stop.

Jordan: Hey, ringtone DJ, I don't wanna hear your tones. Stop showing off, jackass.

Ringtone DJ: Hey, do you like this one? It's "I Wanna 1-2-1 With You."

ripcord

To flee from an awkward situation or boring lecture. Usually involves walking in front of others or in some other way disturbing the peace and making an ass of oneself.

He pulled out the PowerPoint presentation; that was my signal to ripcord.

ripe

Stinky or nasty.

The hamper is pretty ripe.

roach

When a dog lies on its back with all four legs in the air—like a dead cockroach.

Fido is roaching on the couch.

road parrot

To ride on the shoulder of the road in order to avoid long lines and traffic.

Dude, screw traffic. Time to road parrot!

roast

To humorously mock or humiliate someone with a well-timed joke, diss, or comeback.

When Gonzo got drunk, he made fun of John's ugly-ass suit—it was a delicious roast.

robotripping

Drinking a bottle of Robitussin cough syrup (containing DXM), with the intention of hallucinating.

We all stole bottles of Robitussin and went robotripping. I spent most of the night wrapped in the arms of a warm, friendly purple octopus.

rock star parking

Parking up close to the venue being visited.

I don't want to drive. I can't afford to give up my rock-star parking.

roll on
To snitch or divulge private information about a person; in criminal terms, to snitch for some sort of protection or legal incentive.

Inmate 1: Shit, son, why am I in jail? My friend got out on parole!

Inmate 2: Ha, stupid ass, he rolled on you!

roll pennies
Riding on wheels that are less than desirable: too small, ugly, mismatched, trashy, horribly colored, etc.

Shit, that Pinto would be deck if that fool wasn't rollin' pennies!

roll thick
To associate with a large group of people; to travel/go out with a large entourage.

Don't mess with Tyrone. He rolls thick.

rooting
In America it means cheering; in Australia it means having sex.

Jim Courier, the American tennis player, was commenting on a match for Australian television. A female player was close to victory on court, while the players for the next match wanted her to close out the match so they could get on court. Courier said, "There's two guys in the locker room rooting loudly for her."

rudeboy
1. An avid listener of ska music, especially that of "traditional" and "2-tone" waves of ska.

Check out that rudeboy skank to the ska music!

2. Jamaican gangsters; boys who caused trouble and were known as "rude" because of their attitudes.

That rudeboy down the street was just arrested again!

rung bell
When you do something that you can't take back or reverse, as in "You can't unring that bell."

Jan's decision to have a one-night stand is a rung bell.

rust standard
A standard of low or suspect quality; opposite of the "gold standard."

When it comes to objectivity and fairness in news coverage, CNN sets the rust standard.

R

dictionary

sad trombone

Expression of sadness. Describes the sound made by a trombone to illustrate a depressing statement, action, or moment. "Wah waah." Pioneered on the *SNL* skit "Debbie Downer."

Tad: Bjorn, did you show Nell those pictures of your new kitten?

Bjorn: I don't think so. Nell, would you like to see the pictures I have of Sir Fluffles?

Nell: Oh, Bjorn, I can't bear to look at pictures of cats—they only make me think of watching my own Mr. Snowflake waste away due to the effects of feline leukemia.

Tad: Wow . . . sad trombone!

safety buzz

Drinking alcohol so as to have some excuse at a later date for the trouble you might get into.

We can't go to the club until I get my safety buzz at home.

safety date

A person who accompanies you to a friend's or family event to give the appearance that you are seeing people and not isolated from society or to avoid being set up on blind dates by well-meaning friends.

Jack brought a safety date to his aunt's dinner party because his aunt considered herself an accomplished matchmaker.

salty

Feeling dumb or stupid after something happens.

He tried to throw the ball at the catcher's head, but it bounced and hit the batter. He musta felt salty.

mo'urban

sample slut

Somebody who hovers around free sample counters in food stores and/or takes more than one free sample.

Look at that sample slut blocking the bakery counter. She thinks, "Try one" means try one, then try another one, and another one . . .

the sandbox

Middle Eastern nation, particularly one with a vast desert such as Iraq or Saudi Arabia.

Just heard the 224th is headed over to the sandbox.

Santa

The fattest, oldest pimp this side of the North Pole.

Santa has three hoes. Damn that's jolly.

sarcaustic

Sarcasm mixed with a generous helping of bitterness.

Sarcastic, angry, and bitter at the world, and especially men, Noodle is sarcaustic.

sav

Cool, excellent. Short for "savage."

Tad: This band is quite good.

Bo: Yeah, sav!

SBD

Acronym for "silent but deadly." A quiet fart that makes its presence known by a foul odor.

Woo, baby, you blow out another SBD on me or what? Damn!

search engine

A web site that shamelessly endorses other web sites by letting people add their sites to a great big list of sites.

I searched "ancient Egyptian remains" on the search engine and got 14,000 results, mainly consisting of pornography.

see bottoms

Having your last drink of the night. Usually said three quarters of the way down a pint of beer, i.e., when you actually start to see the bottom of the glass. From the expression "bottoms up."

Bartender: Another beer, Jack?

Jack: No. I'm seeing bottoms.

senioritis

A crippling disease that strikes high school seniors. Symptoms include laziness; excessive wearing of track pants, old athletic shirts, sweatpants, athletic shorts, and sweatshirts; lack of studying; repeated absences; and a generally dismissive attitude. The only known cure is a phenomenon known as "graduation."

Jared: Why didn't you study for your math test, Kuhns?

Kuhns: Oh, who studies for a math test anyway? I got senioritis.

September 10th

An old and outdated way of thinking characterized by complacency and self-satisfaction.

Insensitivity and selfishness are so September 10th.

serial chiller

A person who always kicks back, kicks it, relaxes. One who rarely shoulders responsibility and avoids stress and anxiety.

Jake is either grafted to the couch, the backyard hammock, the lounge chair, or the La-Z-Boy . . . or he's still in bed. He's a serial chiller.

Urban Dictionary defines slang as "the ever-evolving bastardization of language as a result of idolization of uneducated celebrities." Urban Dictionary is called a slang dictionary, but it really defines more than just slang; urbandictionary.com contains definitions for all the 2008 U.S. presidential candidates, for example. (Those will come in handy in the voting booth.) Everyone's got their own opinion of what slang is, so Urban Dictionary's definition is broad: Any word you use in everyday speech is welcome.

seven-minute silence

An awkward moment of silence when no one has anything to say that occurs after seven minutes of conversation.

My date and I were chatting really well; then, out of the blue, the seven-minute silence hit. Bummer.

the sex

Hot, awesome, incredibly cool, and, well, sexy.

Hey, that guy's hair is the sex.

sexclusive

Having sex with only one person, yet not dating them exclusively. The ability to date several people while having an understanding with one in particular that they are your only sex partner.

I couldn't have sex with Tito last night because Mike and I are sexclusive.

sexiquette

The rules of etiquette in regards to sex.

It is poor sexiquette to not return the favor.

sexpectation

The state of anticipating or expecting sexual intercourse from a social encounter, be it a date, a party, or a booty call. It describes a period of optimistic waiting that is just shy of a sure thing.

On the ride home from that date, the sexpectation was killing me!

shabby chic
Something (maybe someone, e.g., Joan Collins) that's rather worn out and tattered yet has a touch of understated class.

With her slightly ratty but damn gorgeous Prada handbag, a pair of Vivienne Westwood slacks, and a frayed cashmere sweater, she was definitely shabby chic.

shaka
Hawaiian hand gesture with many meanings. Originally it meant to "hang loose," or to chill and be laid-back. It can be used as a positive reinforcement. If somebody did something good, cool, or righteous, you can give them a shaka as a sign of approval or praise. It can also be used as a welcome/good-bye sign. To make a shaka:

1. Make a loose fist.

2. Extend both your pinky and your thumb.

3. Lightly shake your hand (too fast makes you look retarded or like a tourist, and too slow makes you look stupid).

Eh, shaka brah.

shake the spot
To leave a location.

Man, about to shake the spot.

shero
A female hero; a heroine.

That girl just saved my life! She's my shero!

shiftless
A style of writing that uses only lowercase letters.

e.e. cummings wrote many of his poems in the shiftless style, using no uppercase letters at all.

shocklog
A weblog intended to shock. The term was coined to describe a number of Dutch web sites that have specialized in presenting shocking, irritating, or "irresponsible" material. Shocklogs have become enormously popular in the Netherlands.

In 2006 the shocklog Geenstijl published confidential information on Ernst Wesselius, a member of the justice department in the Netherlands Antilles, along with his erotic writings.

shoot the five
To put your fists up to fight.

Yo, talk all that shit, then shoot the five.

shop naked
To shop for items online; to buy things from an online store.

I think I'm going to save myself a lot of holiday shopping hassles and just shop naked.

shopulent

The phenomenon of increasingly opulent and ornate shopping centers.

The Venetian Hotel's shopping concourse has a canal with gondoliers, frescoes, paintings, and gold trim everywhere; it is utterly shopulent.

shoulder surfing

Someone who looks over your shoulder while you're talking, looking for someone better to talk to.

The shoulder surfer I was just talking to wasn't even listening to my life story!

shuttle plate

Small plate used to transport food from one dish to another. Very useful in large family-style dinners.

Sure, you can try some of my chicken. Send the shuttle plate down here so I can pass you some.

side-button

To hit the ignore button on a cell phone to avoid speaking with someone. Derived from the button on Nextel phones. You know you've been side-buttoned if it rings for a shorter time than usual before going to voice mail.

Mark: Oh no! Greg is calling.

Jessica: Don't answer it!

Mark: Good idea, I'll side-button him.

sidetalk

Quiet conversation that takes place between people who are sitting beside each other during some kind of committee meeting or official gathering. When enough goes on, and as sound grows exponentially, it can be loud enough to distract the chairperson or whomever is speaking, as well as annoy those who want to carry the meeting's agenda forward.

During the meeting, the mayor became so frustrated with all the sidetalk going on between the city councillors, she finally yelled, "Can you all pay attention to what I'm saying for just a second?!"

slap your plastics

To insert contacts in one's eyes.

Slap your plastics and let's go.

sleeper

Outwardly common-looking item that possesses something special or unique inside.

That boring-looking car is a real sleeper with that big turbo hiding under the hood and nary a sticker or scoop to be seen anywhere on it.

sleep working

To work while still sleeping and somehow managing to get the job done. Related to sleepwalking and sleep talking, only you get paid.

Not to be confused with other occupations involving getting paid for being in bed.

The tech-support guys on the night shift were very adept at sleep working; the customers calling in never knew they were talking and typing with their eyes closed.

SMV
Acronym for "sexual market value."

When a person is seen in public with an attractive and charming partner, their SMV goes up, meaning they become more attractive to other potential partners.

snakes on a plane
A simple existential observation that has the same meaning as "Whaddya gonna do?" or "Shit happens." Taken from the Samuel L. Jackson movie of the same name.

Irate Guy: Dude, you just ran into the back of my SUV!

Calm Guy: Snakes on a plane, man. Snakes on a plane.

snap
1. Expression used to convey dismay.

Oh snap, I used too much dynamite.

2. Expression used to convey disbelief.

Oh snap! It's Speedy Gonzalez!

3. Expression used to convey surprise.

Holy snap! I have boobies!

4. Expression used to convey joy.

Snap! She took off her shirt!

snap music
A style of music originating in the Dirty South. Snap music has a slower tempo than crunk music but still talks about clubbin' and strippers. It is characterized by the finger-snap effect in place of the snare drum. Different people take credit for originating this style, including Fabo, D4L, and Dem Franchise Boys.

D4L's hot single "Laffy Taffy" is one of the most popular songs in snap music.

snarky
A witty mannerism, personality, or behavior that is a combination of sarcasm and cynicism. Usually accepted as a complimentary term. Snark is sometimes mistaken for a snotty or arrogant attitude.

Her snarky remarks had half the room on the floor laughing and the other half ready to walk out.

sneeze tease
The body's preparation for a sneeze that is deferred just before climax. The "ah . . . ah . . . ah" without the "choo."

I thought I was going to sneeze during my presentation, but luckily, it was only a sneeze tease.

S

dictionary

snout

Singular or plural reference to cigarettes.

Give us a snout.

snow job

An effort to deceive, overwhelm, or persuade with insincere talk, especially flattery.

The entire presentation was a complete snow job.

S on my chest

Referring to the S on Superman's chest. When someone walks around like they got an S on their chest, they walk around like nothing can harm them or like they're invincible.

Like Captain Save-A-Ho, I got an S on my chest.

soul patch

The patch of hair grown right under the lip. Any self-respecting stylish male has one.

His soul patch was so long, he saved a meal for later in it.

soymanella

Food poisoning from eating contaminated fake meat.

I was puking all night. I bet it was that nasty-ass six-month-old soymanella-infested tofurkey.

spatula

A woman who turns straight men gay.

It starts out OK, but I always turn them over; I'm a spatula.

spim

An online advertising solicitation sent via an instant messaging program, usually containing a link to a web site featuring services such as pornography, credit repair, or prescription drug sales. Like spam, these communications are often sent under the guise of being a message from a friend. The links enclosed may also be used to spread viruses.

Spim: Come check out my hot new web-cam! My sorority sisters and I are about to take a shower together!

spring break

The time of school year where college-aged young adults and some high school students descend upon vacation resorts such as Cabo, Cancun, Miami, and other sunny locales to partake in much debauchery that usually results in hangovers, a burning sensation when urinating, strange discharge coming from various orifices, interesting pictures, and great memories!

Girl 1: Hey, have you heard about the new spring break hot spot?

Girl 2: No, where is it?

Girl 1: Intercourse, Pennsylvania! Amish country! I can't wait to get freaky at the barn raising! MTV is going to be there! I gotta go out and buy an apron to go with my dress!

spring broke

When you're broke because you spent all your money on spring break.

Guy 1: Hey, man, wanna go to a movie or somethin'?

Guy 2: Nah, I'm spring broke. The cash I took to Vegas, stayed in Vegas.

stack loot

To make money, generally a lot of it.

I've been stackin' loot all day, man. Now it's time to unwind.

stall call

Using the bathroom while on the phone.

Caller: Where you at?

Callee: Um, in the bathroom—do you care if I make this a stall call?

static

Tension or strife.

Don't allow your girlfriend to cause static when you're trying to get wasted with your friends.

sticks

Crayons, usually a classic Crayola eight pack.

Yo I'm packin' mad sticks. I'ma put down mad wax in a minute.

stop and chat

When someone stops to engage in a conversation with another while passing them in public. These conversations are short, meaningless, awkward, and mostly unwanted by at least one of the parties involved. Made popular by Larry David on the HBO series *Curb Your Enthusiasm*.

Oh, there's Tom. Don't acknowledge him, he always wants to stop and chat.

street platinum

Selling 100,000 units of independently produced CDs and tapes. Selling mix tapes and original music productions out the back of their ride à la DJ Whoo Kid and 50 Cent before he was signed to a major label. Average cost of a mix tape is $10, and $10 times 100,000 units equals $1,000,000.

My shit went street platinum without the strength of Fiddy or any other major balla hyping my CD.

street spam

Advertisements posted on telephone poles, traffic lights, and other public areas.

Honest, officer, I didn't even see the stop sign! Look at all the street spam all over that corner.

subwoof

To sit in a car with a subwoofer pounding for no other purpose than letting everyone around you know that you have a system.

Brent got a new system. Now he's sitting outside subwoofing.

sucka free

Single-status female. Finally kicking a POS boyfriend to the curb after a long and crappy relationship, usually to the relief of all friends and family.

I'm sucka free and happy as can be!

sucks out loud

Something that is really bad and you just can't bear to watch and or hear it.

Damn, your guitar playing sucks out loud.

SuFi

Otherwise known as the "super finger." The act of holding up the two inner fingers on your hand. Used by comedian Dane Cook. The SuFi is now widely used during road rage.

When a car passes into your lane without a blinker, give him a SuFi salute.

suitcase college

A college or university where many students go back home every weekend.

It'd be easier to tag some Friday-night ass here if this weren't such a suitcase college.

Super Bowl

The only show that makes me eager to watch the commercials.

Did you see the Reno 911 movie trailer during the Super Bowl? That movie's gonna rock!

swagger jacker

A person who steals someone else's flow, lines, jokes, swagger.

Guy 1: Ay, bro, I just spit this whole song.

Guy 2: Na, you didn't, Hova. I heard Biggie say you a swagger jacker.

swang

To steer your car side to side when driving. Mostly done when cruising.

Swang your Cadillac down the street.

swipeout

When you've maxed out all your credit cards.

I can't buy that dress. I've hit a swipeout.

swish

Expression used when a surprising victory or zinger has occurred. Usually accompanied by a two-handed gesture: both arms up, palms forward. Then, swing wrists so that your palms end facing the floor without moving your arms. Do this as you say "swish."

Eric: She hid the beer, but I found it.

Connor: Oh, swish!

table banking

While splitting a check when out with a group, paying the whole tab with your credit card and taking everyone else's cash instead of going to the ATM.

I'm kind of low on cash. Anyone mind if I do some table banking?

table queen

An individual who is highly particular about where they sit in a restaurant and will make a hostess wait while they locate the best table or have the hostess move them if a "better" table becomes available.

My friend is such a table queen, it takes us ten minutes just to sit down.

tag hag

A person who will only wear clothing that is hideously expensive and bears the right tag or label.

She's such a tag hag. She wanted to wear my Versace even though she hates it!

take him/her to the stacks

A term to imply that sexual relations would be desired between a patron and a library employee.

That patron is so hot, I'd take him to the stacks.

take one for the team

The act of someone willingly making a sacrifice for the benefit of others.

There wasn't enough room in the car, so Jerry decided to take one for the team and stayed behind while the rest of us went to the big concert.

dictionary

take the mickey

To make fun of someone or something, often in a mocking or satirical way, or to attempt to fool someone by telling an outrageous story. Often used also to cast doubt on the truth of a statement.

Person 1: You know, the timers on British nuclear bombs were so bad in the '50s, they thought of filling them with chickens to keep them warm enough.

Person 2: What! Are you taking the mickey?

tall tee

An oversized T-shirt that usually reaches down to one's knees. Commonly worn by gangsters and thugs.

I'ma be rockin' my tall tee at tha club tonight.

tax

To steal; to take something without the owner's permission or consent and without any intention of returning it.

Damn, someone broke into my house last night and taxed my TV.

TC

Acronym for "take care."

Thanks for the info. TC.

technosexual

A person who is so deeply enthralled with technology they discuss it with a level of passion that most people reserve for sex. Not always a geek or a nerd, but generally someone who has the latest and greatest everything.

She became so excited about her new laptop and iPhone that her friends knew she must be a technosexual.

techtarded

A person or situation that is technologically impaired.

You can't figure out how to turn on your iPod? How techtarded can you be?

teledildonics

Computer-mediated sexual interaction between the VR presences of two humans. This practice is not yet possible except in the rather limited form of erotic conversation in chat rooms.

Connect to my teledildonics server now, biatch!

television

The early twenty-first-century drug of choice. A shared illusion, making its addicts think they have friends, a life, access to good information, and the critical thinking skills necessary to form valid opinions. Fatal in large doses.

Paul spent the day eating Cheetos and watching television, then had a heart attack in the evening.

tell us how you really feel

An ironic riposte to an emotional or invective-laden tirade, meaning, more or less, "You've achieved the maximum of outrage."

So you say the teacher is a festering, mold-encrusted, reeking squid. Now tell us how you really feel!

testicular fortitude

Balls, guts, intestinal fortitude.

He lacked the testicular fortitude to stand up to his boss.

testiculate

To move hands and arms expressively while talking bollocks.

As he got more and more drunk, not only was he loud, but he was testiculating wildly.

All of the definitions on Urban Dictionary are written by people just like you. If you know a definition that needs to be included, visit urbandictionary.com to add it. Your definition will be reviewed by volunteer editors and will get published on the site. Sounds like a good way to win a Scrabble game.

testosterphone

To make a quick and to-the-point phone call that lasts under thirty seconds.

Let me testosterphone James—it will only take a minute!

tetris

To intricately and carefully pack stuff into a tight space when normally it would not fit; what you have to do to put twenty pounds of shit into a ten-pound bag.

Skeptic: I don't think we can fit the body, the chainsaw, the money bags, and the beer cooler in this little trunk.

Doer: We'll just have to tetris it.

textless

In an email, IM, IRC, SMS, or MUD exchange, temporarily unable to write, as through astonishment. Compare to "speechless" in spoken language.

Person 1: Remember that sick panda at the zoo? She died.

Person 2: . . . I'm textless.

text massage

When one gets a text message when their phone is on vibrate. The phone vibrates and creates a massaging feeling in one's thigh, creating pleasure for the recipient.

T

Job interviewer: What do you think you can offer to the company?

Ryan: Uhhh . . . ahhhhhhhhhhhhh.

Narrator: Ryan cannot control his emotions during his interview because he was receiving a text massage.

textpectation

The anticipation one feels when waiting for a response to a text message.

I just texted her for a date, but now the textpectation is killing me.

textual intercourse

The consummation of a sexual relationship via SMS messages.

Matt and Heather have been having textual intercourse for over a month.

Thanksgiving pants

Pants that are worn in anticipation of eating a huge meal, e.g., Thanksgiving dinner. These pants usually boast an elastic waist to allow some give for that third helping of sweet potato pie.

The girls and I are going to a buffet for dinner, so I'm wearing my Thanksgiving pants.

that's how I roll

A justification for how a person behaves.

Brendan: You can't just go around stealing money from orphans!

Rob: I can, because that's how I roll.

thesaurus

To use the thesaurus for every second word in order to make yourself sound smarter or to take up space and make an essay longer. Teachers see past it very quickly.

"I walked slowly down the street to school" becomes "I sauntered languorously down the boulevard to the establishment of education" when thesaurused.

thespian lesbian

Any straight woman who acts attracted to or performs sexual acts on another woman for a camera or filming, especially for videos like *Girls Gone Wild*.

Janie says she only likes men, but when the camera goes on she is a real thespian lesbian.

thinspiration

Thin + inspiration. A motivational tool like an image, lyrics, poems, quotes, or sayings that inspires you to stay thin.

Kate Moss is my thinspiration.

Third Coast

Dirty South; hip-hop slang for the southeast.

After decades of East Coast/West Coast rap domination, Third Coast artists are becoming the hottest thing in hip-hop.

third joke

A "third joke" is when someone says something funny, someone else feels the need to follow it with something that may or may not also be funny, and then a third person, trying to keep up, follows up with a third quip, which by this point is most definitely no longer funny. It is important for others at this point to call "third joke" out loud to point out the third individual's social error, to embarrass them for killing the funny. A truly unskilled individual can third joke on the second quip.

Bob: And then I said, "That's not my fish!" Ha ha!

Bill: A halibut tale! Ha ha!

Ted: I smell fish! Ha . . . um.

Bob: Third joke, Ted.

thirsty

Too eager to get something (especially play); desperate.

Boy, running up: Ay, girl, whassup? Look, you lookin' real nice, can I get that young number?

Girl, under breath: Thirsty.

thrift

To visit several different thrift shops, secondhand shops, and vintage clothing stores in hopes of buying several items of cheap and unusual clothing.

Girl 1: Hey, where did you get that weird top?

Girl 2: Oh, I found it while thrifting. It was only a dollar.

thunderwear

Underwear for the extremely obese, those who make the earth tremble when they walk. Specifically: thunderbras, thunderthongs, thunderpants.

Three-hundred-and-fifty-pound Herb's thunderwear was big enough to cover the infield at Yankee Stadium.

tiger

A word said condescendingly by someone at least one year older than someone else, often but not exclusively by a retiree to a teenager. It makes fun of the younger person's energetic, unlearned, immature, vicious, aggressive, dynamic persona.

Easy there, tiger.

time traveling

Being so wasted that you have no recollection of a long period of time.

Man, I must have been time traveling. I remember getting to the party last night, but how did I end up in my bed today?

tinfoil hat

An implication that someone believes in supernatural or conspiratorial phenomena. Refers to the stereotype of wearing a hat made from kitchen aluminum foil, with the purpose of shielding the wearer's brain from mind control/surveillance by various supernatural or conspiratorial organizations.

Mike is still talking about space aliens? He must have left his tinfoil hat at home.

tip

To cruise in your car slowly down a street and swerve left to right. Often done in the South.

Yeah, I still be tippin' in my rydz on dem 44z.

titsicle

Nipples that are hard due to cold.

I walked outside without a jacket and got instant titsicles.

tits on a bull

Someone or something that is absolutely useless.

Brian is a douche bag. He's clearly as useful as tits on a bull.

tits up

Broken; dead in the water; floating.

Well, that project really went tits up.

tl;dr

Too long; didn't read.

tl;dr . . . Why don't you give up on your unabridged edition of War and Peace *or at least stop posting it here?*

TMI

Acronym for "too much information"—way more than you need or want to know about someone.

John: I have mad chafing on my balls.

Frank: Uh, TMI.

TomKitten

Nickname given to Tom Cruise and Katie Holmes's baby, Suri.

After the TomKitten was born, Tom Cruise ate the placenta.

tonk

Ghetto for "strong" or "muscular." Adopted from the unbreakable Tonka trucks back in the day.

Don't mess with him. He is tonk.

tonorrow

Either tonight or tomorrow.

Go away, Mom, I'll try to get a job tonorrow.

tool up

Grab your pistol; get your gun.

Yo, son, tool up. Dem boyz comin'.

top-up music

The kind of music that you listen to only when the convertible top and all windows are up. Also known as "closet music," it is the kind of music that you don't want anyone to know that you like.

The Black Eyed Peas came on Hits 1,

but the top was down so I couldn't listen. BEP is my favorite top-up music!

toy soldier

A friend who's willing to go out and ride with you, no matter what the situation may be. A friend who has your back and is willing to give his life to ensure your protection (in essence, a friend who acts like a bodyguard).

My dawg G-War is my toy soldier. He always got my back.

trainspotting

Listening to or observing a mixed set of tracks. DJs and clubbers who tend to observe and analyze the method and sound of the DJ are known as trainspotters.

The records skipped in the club because there were so many trainspotters crowding around and shoving in the booth.

trainsurfing

Riding a train any way except inside the train cars. Usually done by hanging onto the back, sides, or top of the train while the train is in motion. The equivalent of ghost riding cars.

There are some awesome videos on YouTube of trainsurfing.

tramp stamp

A tattoo above a woman's butt.

Her pants were so low cut, you could see her tramp stamp.

tranny

1. Transvestite.
2. Transsexual.
3. Photographic transparency.
4. Transit van.

Damn. I left the trannies of the trannies in the back of the tranny.

trap

The area where drug deals are carried out. Also: "trap house."

The dope boy is in the trap tonight.

treeware

Documents made of paper, like an anablog, in contrast to electronic documents.

Print out the treeware and we can send it via snail mail.

tricked out

Heavily accessorized.

At her coronation, the queen was all tricked out in brocade, ermines, and the crown jewels.

trippin'

Crazy.

Bitch, you be trippin'!

trout pout

Lips with collagen injected to make them plumper, particularly when it goes wrong and they look like a fish.

Leslie has got a trout pout!

trowler

A woman wearing a huge amount of makeup.

I bet she put that on with a trowel. She's a trowler.

truthanize

1. To brilliantly inform someone of a harsh truth that they were either ignorant of or tried with everything they have to ignore. The resulting truth leaves the liar impotent, powerless. Like euthanize, but with the truth.

Man, the Scooter Libby indictment and the lack of WMD in Iraq fully truthenized Rumsfeld and Cheney.

2. To call someone out on a huge lie.

Dude, at the end of A Few Good Men, *Jack Nicholson gets truthanized.*

truthiness

The quality of stating concepts one wishes or believes to be true, rather than the facts. Origin: Stephen Colbert, *The Colbert Report.*

That Fox News report didn't have all of the facts, but it had a certain truthiness to it.

tryptophanatic

One who eats until they are engorged . . . and then proceeds to eat even more, usually resulting in a turkey coma. A glutton—but a happy glutton nonetheless.

Yeah, I was a total tryptophanatic over the holidays. I think I slept for about thirty hours after I ate that second turkey.

tryptophan coma

The feeling of exhaustion one feels after Thanksgiving dinner due to the large amounts of tryptophan ingested through overeating.

I'll see you the day after Thanksgiving, assuming that I've snapped out of my tryptophan coma by then.

tune my guitar to sad

This phrase is used to either be emo or to mock an emo kid. It describes the classic emo musician and mocks the ever-so-sad emo song.

Person 1: I ran out of black eyeliner this morning, and my new hair isn't as black as I wanted it.

Person 2: This is such a cruel world . . .

Bystander: Aw, I'm gonna tune my guitar to sad.

tune wedgie

A song or advertising jingle annoyingly stuck in your head. Also: "ear worm."

No, don't sing the Barney theme song! You'll give me a tune wedgie.

tween

A girl age about nine to fourteen. Too old for toys, but too young for boys. Very easy to market to, tweens will usually follow any fashion trend set for them.

Mary-Kate and Ashley Olsen's main fan base are all tweens.

twixter
A person between the ages of eighteen and twenty-five and even beyond, who have become a part of a distinct and separate life stage, a strange, transitional never-never land between adolescence and adulthood in which people stall for a few extra years, putting off the iron cage of adult responsibility that constantly threatens to crash down on them.

Yeah, my friend is twenty-six, still lives at home with the 'rents, and parties all week. Ah, the life of a twixter.

typeative/typeractive
Describes someone who sends long emails or instant messages. "Talkative" for the IM generation.

Are you busy at work today? Because you haven't been very typeative.

U

u

Shorthand for the word "you." Commonly used on the Internet.

u cumn ovr 2day 4 sx?

ubersexual

A male who is similar to a metrosexual but displays the traditional manly qualities such as confidence, strength, and class—leaving no doubt as to his sexual orientation.

Bono is the world's leading ubersexual.

unbeweavable

Fake hair that is way over the top.

That girl had like fifty different colors up in there—that's unbeweavable.

uncomfortafull

So full it's uncomfortable.

I ate so much for dinner that I'm uncomfortafull.

United States of Canada

All the blue states that voted for Kerry in the 2004 election; the states that are so embarrassed that Bush won the election they wish they belonged to Canada instead.

After the election, a new map was drawn showing the United States of Canada and Jesusland.

unleaded

Decaffeinated coffee. Crap that tastes like coffee but doesn't give you a caffeine buzz. Waste of time.

Waitress: What can I get you?

Customer: Coffee.

Waitress: Leaded or unleaded?

unobtainium

An imaginary unavailable material used humorously to solve otherwise impossible problems; an item of unaffordable price.

Of course, it would have to be made of pure unobtainium to work.

unpack

To take a massive dump.

Brian: All right, guys, I'm gonna go unpack. Talk to you later.

Norm: Yeah, it'll probably make you feel a lot better.

unpimp

To destroy something that has been overly accessorized.

Chris spent $5,000 and two years putting all that bling and fins on his Corolla, but it took his ex-girlfriend just ten minutes and a crow bar to unpimp his ride.

unportant

The opposite of important. Also used to describe somebody who is merely pretending that you are important.

Your call is very unportant to us.

unprotected sleep

Turning off your alarm clock and immediately going back to sleep; risking not waking up for a job, class, or other daily task.

I'm lucky that I didn't miss my final exam after having thirty minutes of unprotected sleep.

unschooling

The practice of an individual who does not attend school—instead choosing to travel, write, play, run, build things, volunteer, and learn about the world free of grades, subjects, periods, and "school hours."

Where most schooling puts the emphasis on what needs to be learned, unschooling puts the emphasis on who is doing the learning.

urban amish

Someone who has none of the technological devices that have become a part of our daily lives, such as television, microwave, gaming platform, or home computer.

I'm going to Ohio for a visit with the urban amish relatives. Where's my Game Boy?

urban cougar

An older woman, typically in her early thirties to mid-forties, who has abandoned traditional rules of romantic engagement and taken as her mission the seduction of as many game young men as she can possibly handle. Also just "cougar."

Some urban cougar with a boob job tried to buy me a drink last night.

U

dictionary

The urban cougar, also known as the "cougar," is on the prowl and preying on younger men. The adjective is "cougarlicious"—and a young cougar, a woman in her late twenties or early thirties, is a "puma." The young male, the object of the cougar's affections, is a "cougee."

urst

Acronym for "unresolved sexual tension."

Me and my math teacher, we have some urst.

utilize

A substitute for the word "use" to be employed when you want to make something sound more important or difficult than it really is.

We utilize an alphabetical schematic to organize our records.

Translation: We file documents alphabetically.

V

vacationship

A long-distance relationship in which the couple only gets together for idyllic vacation-like excursions, therefore avoiding the "real-life" issues of dating.

She met this guy online last summer, but he lives in Austin and doesn't want to move, so they've struck up this very intense vacationship.

Valentine's Day

The reason so many people are born in November.

I was born in November because my parents celebrated Valentine's Day.

val pal

A Valentine's Day partner to give and receive gifts from at school.

I love my val pal.

value add

A business euphemism for "the reason I'd like you to think I'm useful."

My value add on this project is to leverage best-known-methods (BKMs) to focus on strategies leveraging core competencies moving forward synergistically to achieve our mutual business objectives.

vaulted

When a secret or an important piece of information is confirmed safe with the person you have entrusted it to.

Scott: Sarah, I want to tell you that I actually have a Spice Girls doll collection . . . and I brush their hair while listening to "Wannabe."

Sarah: Don't worry, Scott. It's totally vaulted.

vegi-curious

One who is considering the vegetarian lifestyle, but has yet to make a commitment to it.

No sausage on my half of the pizza; I'm vegi-curious.

velocitized

Accustomed to a rate of speed.

I got off the freeway onto a 25 mph street and got pulled over. I didn't even notice I was speeding because I was velocitized.

vitamin v

Viagra. Because some people take it like it's a vitamin.

My wife and I are planning a hot night; got to take my vitamin v.

vlog

Video log. A journalistic video documentation on the web of a person's life, thoughts, opinions, and interests. Can be topical and timeless, instructional and entertaining. The main objective is to communicate on a personal level with your audience.

Zadi decided that setting up a daily vlog was the best way to show the sun setting in the west to her friends living in the east.

voicejail

The loop of options one gets stuck in when trying to navigate voice mail settings.

I tried changing my phone greeting and I got stuck in voicejail.

> **VEGI-CURIOUS**
>
> Sometimes the vegi-curious turn into "flexitarians"— people who mostly eat veggies, but aren't too uptight about eating meat occasionally. You could also call that a "faketarian" diet.

W

w/e
Whatever.

OK u know what? Stop messin' with me. Forget it . . . w/e!

w00t
An expression of joy and excitement.

I just got an A on my test. w00t!

wage slave
Someone who earns only enough at their job to pay for basic expenses. Sometimes referred to as "working poor."

Retirement savings?! I'm a wage slave. I make $5 an hour.

wag the dog
When something of secondary importance improperly takes on the role of something of primary importance.

Concentrate on the dog wagging his tail, not on the fact that the tail might wag the dog.

wagwan
Bastardization of "What's going on?"

Wagwan, my brotha?

wake and bake
To toke up right after you wake up.

Morning, Drew. I got ten dollars. Feel like a wake and bake?

the walk of shame
Walking home still wearing your clothes from the night before after staying over at a guy or girl's house you met a party.

She took the walk of shame, still wearing her dress and heels, at 6 a.m.

wallet salad

Paper currency of any denomination.

I forgot to hit the ATM. Got any wallet salad on you?

WAM

Acronym for "walking around money." Money given to you by your sugar daddy/sugar momma for you to spend freely.

What, you're out of cash? Why isn't your man givin' you any WAM? My man gives me WAM all the time because he knows he won't get any booty otherwise.

wangsta

Wannabe gangsta.

Bob is a wangsta.

wantaway

A player in soccer who no longer wishes to play for his current club.

Nottingham Forest are in talks with Southampton over their wantaway defender.

way

Hella, very, totally, extremely, etc.

That car is way cool!

WD55

An acronym for "windows down, 55 miles an hour." A primitive form of air conditioning most helpful to '60s and '70s Volkswagen Bug pilots.

Air conditioning? Hell no! We got WD55!

wdym

Acronym for "what do you mean?" or "whatever do you mean?"

Tom: Yeah, isn't that awesome?

Nic: Wait, wdym?

Tom: You should have been listening!

weak sauce

Lame or boring.

You mean the Phish concert tickets are sold out? Weak sauce, dude.

webcest

Everything depraved, dirty, and otherwise morally outrageous that has become generally available thanks to the Internet.

Webcest is when you start putting your undergarments on the scanner and posting the pictures on pro-anorexia LiveJournal communities.

weekend lag

A condition affecting the body's circadian clock, similar to jet lag, but instead stemming from altering one's sleep hours over a weekend of hard partying and drinking rather than from a long flight.

Frank: Shit, I missed fluid dynamics again. Monday morning classes are so rough. It feels like it is 7 p.m. What time is it?

Jason: It's only 8 a.m.

Brad: Dude, that's a serious case of week-end lag. Drink some fluids and stop hitting the riverboat casino so hard in P-town.

weekend warrior

A person who has a boring rat race job and compensates by being irresponsible during the weekend.

I am a weekend warrior and I like to party, but I can't because my life sucks. Except for the weekends.

weigh grams

To live poorly on little money. Refers to poor, low-level cocaine dealers who sell low quantities.

I remember back when Sheila was just a ho. Back then, she used to hang out with me when I weighed grams. Now, a cut has to hit double platinum before she rides.

wenis

The skin on your elbow.

Hey, Dan! Your wenis is showing!

whack-off light

A flashlight with an internal magnet and coil; marketed as a light without batteries to go dead. Performs poorly and requires a vigorous whacking-off motion to make the magnet generate as much light as a candle.

The batteries in my Maglite were dead so I had to use my whack-off light.

whale tail

The shape formed when a G-string rides up high over a woman's pants or skirt.

Oh my god, look at that butt! Her whale tail is showing so high!

what

In hop-hop, often used as a sort of taunt after a proclamation has been made.

South side runnin' this bitch! What!

whatever humps your camel

Synonym to "whatever floats your boat"; do whatever you want.

Friend: What do you wanna do later?

Me: Whatever humps your camel.

what's crackin'?

A greeting, synonymous with greetings such as "What's going on?"

Hey man, what's crackin'?

W

what's with the socks

A term to ask about the new occurrences in the life of a friend, instead of "What's up?"

John: Hey, Joe, what's with the socks?

Joe: Plain old white ones today.

wheel

Trying to pick up a girl.

I've totally been wheeling this chick from work.

where y'at

A greeting in New Orleans. Reply with, "What it is." If you give the wrong response, the initiator will know you are not local.

Person 1: Where y'at?

Person 2: What it is.

whip

A nice car, usually expensive.

Damn, check out that tight whip! That's them Gs right there!

Time magazine cited "wikiality" as one of their Buzzwords of 2006. That's good news for Stephen Colbert, who coined the term. He also introduced "truthiness," which was named Word of the Year for 2006 by Merriam-Webster.

WIKIALITY

ud

wi-five

A high-five that doesn't involve any actual contact, normally over a long distance where a real high-five isn't possible. Mix of "wireless" and "high-five."

Iain (yelling across the room): Dude, that mess was the pwnz. Wi-five, brosef.

Eric (in response): You need to chill with that nano shit, son.

wii-kend

A weekend devoted exclusively to playing a Nintendo Wii.

Hey, I just ordered a Wii on Amazon.com. It arrives Friday, so I'm going to have one sweet Wii-kend! :D

wiitard

Someone who causes damage or injury to him- or herself, other people, or objects by incorrectly operating the controller of a Nintendo Wii. This includes forgetting or underestimating one's surroundings while using wild gestures, overexertion, or the inability to keep a firm grasp on the remote and launching it at high speeds.

Mandy forgot her family was in the room, acted like a wiitard, and hit her brother in the face.

wikiality

Reality as decided on by majority rule. Based on Wikipedia's "majority

mo'urban

rule" fact. Featured on *The Colbert Report*, July 31, 2006.

The population of elephants in Africa has tripled in the past six months. We know this to be true, despite the absence of facts to back up this opinion. "Vandalizing" the Wikipedia entry to reflect this wikiality is a perfectly valid thing to do.

wikillectual

One whose major knowledge base appears to have been garnered from Wikipedia and its related projects.

Rob concealed his status as a wikillectual once he finally received his wi-fi PDA/cell phone, though those with whom he engaged in intellectual sparring sessions often commented on his overactive bladder, as he constantly ran to the bathroom in order to query the site privately.

wikilobbying

The act of paying others money to edit Wikipedia entries in order to cast the employer's company, product, or point of view in a better light. Coined by Stephen Colbert of *The Colbert Report*. When money determines Wikipedia entries, reality becomes a commodity.

IBM could throw some of their money at perception and make their product "objectively better," then Microsoft can just fire their cash cannons back and we're off to the races. This is the essence of wikilobbying.
—*Stephen Colbert*

wiking off

The practice of reading essentially random Wikipedia pages for entertainment or as a procrastination technique; intellectual masturbation.

Quit wiking off and get back to work!

wild

To go crazy, or do something extreme. Also: "wild out."

Yo, she put him on punishment for three months. She wildin'.

window breaker

An item (usually electronic) left in the car that is worth breaking the window to steal.

Yo, dude, don't leave that iPod in the car. It's a window breaker.

wing nut

A political extremist; usually applied to reactionary conservatives and religious fundamentalists.

That wing nut Senator Tom Colburn (R-OK) called for the death penalty for abortion doctors and sought to investigate "rampant lesbianism" in Oklahoma's public schools.

with legs

In a restaurant, a to-go order.

I will take that order with legs.

W

woodpusher

A term used by rollerbladers to define skateboarders.

Woodpushers suck ass.

wordanista

A person who spends their life telling others what is or is not a word, based on what they have read in books. Coined by Steven Colbert.

I know you wordanistas love to say "funner" is not a word, but it is. I looked it up in my gut, and that's the truth.

word out

A way to mark the end of a conversation and note your departure. Opposite of "word up."

Dude, I gotta run, word out.

word vomit

A point in a conversation where you say something that you really didn't mean to.

I told Robin that I saw Mike with some girl at the movie theater last night. It just came out of my mouth like word vomit.

workmare

A nightmare that is derived directly from your place of employment, including your job, coworkers, duties, and/or responsibilities.

The other night I had a workmare where I botched my presentation and got fired— kept me up half the night.

wrap rage

Fit of anger induced by trying to open hard-to-open plastic packaging like the kind they sell cheap consumer electronics or household items in. May result in injury.

Ironically, he got so caught up in wrap rage that he almost sliced off his finger using a screwdriver to open the X-Acto knife package.

WTF

Acronym for "What the fuck."

After a heavy night of drinking, John exclaims, "WTF, I can't find my wallet!"

WWILF

Acronym for "What was I looking for?" Often used while wasting time surfing online with no results.

Yikes! I've been surfing online for seven hours and everybody's mad at me, plus I haven't found anything useful or important. WWILF?

WTF

"WTF" is one of many Internet acronyms defined on urbandictionary.com. Related words include "omg" (oh my god), "lol" (laugh out loud), "lqtm" (laughing quietly to myself, the alternative to "lol"), "rofl" (rolling on the floor laughing), "lmao" (laughing my ass off), "stfu" (shut the fuck up), "ftw" (for the win), and "bbq" (barbecue). There's a lot of laughing and barbecuing on the Internet.

y/n

A parody of the old DOS programs people used back in the day. It means yes/no, and some geeks still use it when they ask questions.

You want me to send you that file y/n?

yadadamean

Bay Area slang for "You know what I'm sayin'?" Other variations include "yadadaimsayin'" and "yadada I'm talkin bout?"

The bay gets hyphy, yadadamean?

ya rly!

Yeah, really. Response to "o rly?"

Juan: o rly?

Diaz: ya rly!

yinz

Pittsburguese for "you guys."

Jamie asked his companions, "Where are yinz goin'?"

yoink

An exclamation that, when uttered in conjunction with taking an object, immediately transfers ownership from the original owner to the person using the word, regardless of previous property rights.

Though I cherished my automobile, I had to purchase a new one when my second cousin came up from behind me and politely exclaimed, "yoink" while taking my car keys.

yolked

Muscular. Cut.

LL was hella yolked in S.W.A.T.

yo' mama

1. A phrase used as a formal declaration of defeat. For example: "Kenneth replied 'yo, mama' when he realized he could not counter his opponent's point."

Amy: You're so ugly!

Gwen: Yeah, well so's yo' mama!

2. The principal part of a "yo' mama" joke, usually entailing a description of your mother being so "something" that "something" occurred as a result.

Yo' mama so fat, the last time she saw 90210 was on a scale!

Yo' mama so dumb, she thought a quarterback was a refund.

yo' mama reflex

To use "yo' mama" jokes without any intention to and without any thought process.

Jenny: Oh my god. There's a dog on fire outside!

Harold: Yo' mama on fire outside!

Jenny: Where?!

Kenny: Relax, Jenny. That's only his yo' mama reflex.

Harold: That's only yo' mama's yo' mama reflex!

you got got

You've been had; you've been tricked.

Person 1: Hey, man, what about our deal?

Person 2: Heh! You got got!

you got served

Another way of saying "You just got owned" or "Pwned!" A slang expression that is usually used when someone proves that they are better than someone else.

You can't understand the meaning of the Torah and why Moses was an amazing leader of the Jews. I'm sorry, Yaakov, but you just got served by Jewish heritage.

youniverse

The entirety of creation that relates to one specific narcissistic individual. Used to indicate that a particular person has knowledge only of him- or herself—their universe consists only of them.

If you moved outside of your youniverse for five seconds you'd understand that people aren't homeless by choice.

YouTube lunch

Watching videos on YouTube, or any general Internet time-wasting on a lunch break.

Elliot: Fancy going for a pizza?

Ralph: No, I'm thinking of just pulling a YouTube lunch.

yupscale

Affluent in an ostentatiously "hip" sort of a way; a combination of "yuppie" and "upscale."

My neighborhood is becoming more and more yupscale every day—I can't take a walk to the liquor store anymore without tripping over some BoBo with a thousand-dollar stroller and a Prada tote full of organic produce.

zamboni

A piece of cloth (e.g., handkerchief, sock, underwear, T-shirt) that is used to clean up any and all spills in a college dorm room.

Oh crap, I just spilled my beer. Get the zamboni!

ze

A gender-neutral pronoun. It refers to someone who does not fit into gender binary.

Ze is wearing such a cute shirt!

Zidane

To head-butt someone in the chest during a crucial moment. Also: "go Zidane on."

Player 1: Give me the ball.

Player 2: No.

Player 1: Don't make me Zidane you.

zip-block

To get stuck halfway when trying to zip a zipper.

Tom: You ready to go?

Gerry: Hold up. I'm zip-blocked.

the zone

A state of mind that can be reached with little difficulty. When you reach the zone, your mind is 100 percent focused on what you are doing and you have a massive increase in performance.

I reached the zone and I shaved three seconds off my lap time.

zoom zoom

Fast, zippy, fun, aerodynamic, stylish. Coined from Mazda car commercials.

That's a zoom-zoom ride you have there.

zoom zoom zoom

An expression that follows a particularly good but lighthearted insult in order to emphasize the caliber of the remark. It is similar to the way that a person would use the word "burn." Popularized in the television show *Scrubs,* where it is often accompanied by a short "zoom, zoom, zoom" dance.

Guy 1: Dude, you're pathetic because you've never really satisfied a woman!

Guy 2: Oh, really? Well, you might want to check that with your mom! Ohhhh! Zoom zoom zoom!

dictionary

Photo: Hope Harris Photography

Aaron Peckham started Urban Dictionary in 1999 as a freshman at Cal Poly, San Luis Obispo. He graduated six years later with a degree in computer science and fluency in slanglish—the language Urban Dictionary teaches you how to speak. He gets his kicks watching *The Colbert Report* and *Reno 911*, biking, juggling, and reading urbandictionary.com.

Today Aaron is a software engineer in Silicon Valley and San Francisco.

apeckham.com